## The Definitive Guide to
## Building **Seven-Figure Sales**

# MARK EVANS

**Stafford Street Press**

ISBN      978-1-5445-0535-0  *Hardcover*
          978-1-5445-0533-6  *Paperback*
          978-1-5445-0534-3  *Ebook*

*To My Girls*

# CONTENTS

*If you don't set a baseline standard for what you'll accept in life, you'll find it easy to slip into behaviors and attitudes or a quality of life that's far below what you deserve.*

—Tony Robbins

# INTRODUCTION

Let me start by saying, I should have never written a book. Well, at least that's what I told myself for long months and thousands of words pounded out at my dining room table, office, local coffee shop, or wherever else I could squeeze some time in.

See, I should never have written a book because I'm not an author. Authors are people who went to a fancy school, studied Shakespeare and the Classics. They've spent years refining their craft, submitting essays, and smoking pipes in wood-paneled rooms on Harvard Square.

That's what I used to think.

But, throughout the years watching my family's businesses mature and working for some of the fastest moving and growing companies in the United States, I saw some things that I couldn't keep quiet about anymore.

These companies don't multiply because they got lucky or made a viral cat video. Businesses and salespeople accelerate because they're intentional about business and sales.

I've got a soft spot in my heart for small business. I remember being four years old, and my family loading up our brown station wagon with my three sisters and our worldly possessions.

Little did I know that my parents had mortgaged everything to pursue their version of the American Dream. A Dream that looked like a one-employee print shop in southeastern Wisconsin, four hours away from everyone we knew and all of our extended family.

My dad had grown up in the printing business with his father and brothers (he's the oldest of 15 kids!), and while the partnerships had always worked out pretty well, he and my mom were determined to do it on their own.

So they shoved all their chips into the center of the table and bought a small print shop with older equipment and an even older employee that they "inherited."

Call it foreshadowing, but the first day there my younger sister Beth almost electrocuted herself by thinking her hair barrette was a key and a wall electrical outlet was a lock! Then, no less than 20 minutes later, Beth fell down the creaky steps that led to the boiler. Imagine being in town for a few hours and the Evans tribe was already familiar with the Emergency Room staff.

Fast forward 30 years later and my parents savor their well-earned retirement. As they should. They built a very successful operation, were a cornerstone of community involvement, and a fixture in the business community. I'm really proud of them.

Because of that upbringing, I see every salesperson as part "business owner"—no matter if they're a solopreneur or on a large team at a Fortune 500 company. If you're in sales, you're a small business owner. You're responsible for the success of *your* book of business, just like business owners like my dad are responsible for the success of their business.

I know I started by saying I shouldn't have written a book, but what I lack in literary prose I make up for in enthusiasm and a willingness to share everything I've got. Ready to keep going?

This book is for:

1. People who are new to sales
2. Veteran salespeople
3. Business owners

If you're starting in sales, let me congratulate you. You're entering the highest earning profession there is! The opportunity to be world-class and make a fortune has never been better. This book will help you get there. And it's the book I sure as hell wish I had when I started in my first professional sales gig years ago.

If you're a veteran salesperson, chances are you need a little shot in the arm! We all do. Sales is a tough gig, and you need encouragement just as much as you need oxygen. So if you're trying to grind out a quota, maximize your commission plan and grow your sales career, I have the tools and tactics you're going to love and be able to use immediately. I also know how hard it can be to make action happen. This book will serve as a nice dose of enthusiasm.

If you're a business owner, you're in for a treat. If you put the strategies to work in this book, you can have a sales team that produces consistent results allowing you more freedom in your organization. These systems don't work on their own and need to be implemented with confidence and ruthlessly adhered to if you want to make some real headway.

Business owners are the backbone of the economy and the driver of growth. I know firsthand that an increase in sales doesn't show up on Wall Street or earn a mention in Forbes. An increase in sales means the difference between growing or dying. It's the difference between offering your employees a pay increase or having to let them go. It's the difference between buying new equipment or getting pushed out by bigger competitors. See for business owners, sales aren't just numbers. Sales are the absolute lifeblood of your organization. It's the difference between pursuing your dream or having to go work for someone else.

Truth be told, this book is for people like you and I who know we'll have to work hard *and* smart to see results. It's for people who keep their eyes and ears open—people who want to leverage their true potential to create a life of extraordinary proportions.

It's for new salespeople, salespeople who are *not* where they want to be, and people who *are* where they want to be but know the value of sharpening their swords. It's for sales that's business to business and business to consumer, nationwide and local, big teams and small teams. It's for people who sell refrigerators and software and cat meme T-shirts. It's for people in big fancy offices and people working out of their basements. It's for CEOs and sales leaders who either grow their business via sales or they go *out* of business.

In short, this book is for people who actually give a shit about their company, their success, and their future.

So welcome. And, thanks for picking up this book. Honestly, I'm honored.

My name is Mark Evans and I wrote this book with a lot of help from my wife, Katie. I'm a millennial that's sold something (well, lots of things actually) in this decade. I've managed new grads and baby boomers. I've made over six figures since I was twenty-four and am responsible for adding millions of dollars in revenue and developing sales systems that work. I love my wife, mow my lawn while drinking a beer, spend my summers training for triathlons, and believe pure happiness is making my two daughters laugh.

This book is a collection of good advice and hard-earned lessons that I've picked up and learned from mentors, books, seminars, and thousands of hours trying to refine my craft. Let's be honest. Personal development can be boring, expensive, irrelevant, terribly time-consuming, or worse—all the above. This book is hopefully anything but.

I'm far from perfect and I'm not even close to where I believe my potential is. I've made a mountain of mistakes, but I'll keep it real because we are all normal people.

I know that whatever your soul wants or needs to learn, it will latch onto. So highlight this book and write down what's helpful to you. We only have so much mental bandwidth, so do yourself a favor and make it easy to remember.

This book is for you and your future.

# CHAPTER 1

# MY STORY

From third grade until middle school I had to make "the walk." Cutting across the playground during the middle of the day may not sound like much, but it might as well have been the Appalachian Trail.

"The Walk" was a walk to the Resource Room—a special part of the school run by devoted teachers for kids that struggled and needed remedial help. There was no way to hide the fact you were going to the Resource Room. At my small Catholic school, nothing was a secret. I remember how obvious it was when it was time for math, and my teacher gave me that all-knowing and painfully obvious nod of the head.

I'd unceremoniously collect my things as the entire class watched and knew where I was headed. For the next hour, God Bless that resource aide's heart, I received one-on-one help so I'd be more confident and feel less challenged.

Reliving the memory of the Resource Room is enough to bring back real feelings of embarrassment and shame, even 20+ years later. Needless to say, if you placed a bet on whether or not I'd be "successful" by age 30, I wasn't a sure thing.

My high school and early college years were characterized by lots of basketball, weekend partying with friends and the usual shenanigans of Midwestern kids who live in the frozen tundra and don't have much better to do besides drink.

Luckily my life found real purpose when I met my wife during my fourth year of college. My college house was hosting a Halloween party and Katie, my now wife, just so happened to be visiting friends at my school from her college across the state. She dressed as a 1920s flapper and I dressed like an old school basketball player—short shorts and all. We hit it off immediately and a year later we were engaged. That same week of our engagement, I graduated from college, we moved into our first apartment together, and I accepted my first "real" job.

I was ready to show the world my sales glory. But the company I was hired to work for was going through a tough time.

The Great Recession was upon us and the sector I chose to enter, Commercial Printing (due to my family's background I assumed it was an "easy" fit), was struggling. On my third day, they ended up laying off 40 percent of the workforce. To this day I have no idea why they hired me or didn't lay me off three days later despite the significant layoffs.

Unfortunately, things kept getting worse. I was instructed to follow the General Manager and watch what he did for the next three weeks. It was awkward for him, and it was awkward for me. There was zero training. I'd watch him do some work, answer a few emails, and repeat this cycle for 8 to 9 hours. It took everything in me to not fall asleep on the 1970s patterned chair I sat in.

After a couple of months in an environment lacking in motivation and enthusiasm, I got another sales job in the medical device industry and unceremoniously gave my resignation to the General Manager. I left my company-issued computer and old business cards on my desk and ran. Few things in life have felt better than that sweet taste of fresh air after giving my notice.

I worked at my next job selling medical devices for about a year until I had a life-changing conversation with a good friend of my father-in-law's at a local diner over coffee and a greasy omelet. Basically, I was looking for my next opportunity, and he said he could use me. Whether I was hired because of my enthusiasm or family connection (I know it wasn't because of my couple years of sales experience!), I'll never know. But I do know that over the next five years, my life completely changed.

Thanks to Tim, Pete (you'll hear more about him later), Kermit, Bob and Laura, I became a better salesperson and man. Essentially, I grew up. I also have to give a shout out to JD, a fellow sales guy who sold three or four times what I did every year but motivated me like no other, and showed me what's possible if you work hard.

Within my first year, I was making a six-figure income thanks to hard work, the right industry, and a commission package that motivated my money-hungry appetite. My wife was expecting our first daughter, and if that doesn't motivate you, I don't know what does.

The next years were the same—sales and more sales! I loved winning, learned a ton about sales, and was in a constant stretch zone. I also was quickly promoted, so I had the honor of learning how to manage a sales team at a young age.

From there, I took my first real risk. I left this comfortable job where I was making great money, had built great connections, and showed no signs of slowing down. An opportunity at a tech startup glimmered like a shiny penny on the street and I wanted to be in. If you want big rewards you have to take big risks, right?

While I was attracted to this cool thing, it wasn't a great fit. I knew I didn't jive from the get-go. So now what? I didn't regret leaving my old job, but I didn't know what to do next.

I turned to my neighbor—a man who has grown a business from his kitchen table to a $100M company in less than 15 years. I asked for advice. He'd taken some big risks in life, and I was looking for direction. Instead, he told me his company was looking for someone like me and he told me to apply. Fast forward, and I entered an incredible leadership position where I excelled. The company was growing fast so I had exposure to world-class marketing and business systems. I also received training opportunities that threw gas on my personal development fire.

But I had a secret. I knew I was playing small, and I was terrified of taking another risk, so I silenced the voices in my head that told me to level up.

Those voices kept telling me to go out on my own. Take a risk and be in control. My dad and his dad and his dad before him were entrepreneurs. When would it be my turn, I thought?

Eventually, those nagging voices turned into courage and I started to believe I could do it. I thought I had a message to share with others that sales today demand a *new* standard. As I like to say, **"Raise your Standards. Raise your Sales."**

So here we are today. I consult for and train companies and individuals of all shapes and sizes who want to build seven-figure sales teams. And regardless of their shape and size, sales boils down to the Standards I introduce in this book.

I honestly couldn't care less if you went to the "Resource Room" as a kid, have been fired from a sales job, or if you've never really had success in selling. It doesn't matter and it doesn't count. What matters now is that by reading this book you've shown me that you want something more for yourself. Congratulations. This won't be easy, but it will be worth it.

## CHAPTER 2

# WHY SALES?

There are thousands of different jobs you could've chosen in hundreds of different industries. And in many of these industries, there is no shortage of opportunity. So, with the infinite amount of options, why did you choose sales?

Think about it.

With all of the options out there, why sign up for a gig where, more often than not, you're going to be told "*No*"?

Maybe you chose sales for the freedom it provides or the money you could potentially make? Or, you're good at talking to people? Or you fell into it without even realizing it? Or you feel like your product can genuinely help people? Regardless of *how* you got into sales, *how* you're in sales at this very moment is far more critical.

So, why are you in sales?

I'm genuinely interested in your answer. And keep in mind, it needs to be real, and it needs to be compelling.

**I am in sales because:**

I won't sugarcoat it for you. Sales is a tough gig. But you probably already know this.

I often ask anyone who wants to be on my sales team, "What's going to get you out of bed on a cold and snowy day in February?" If I get anything less than a solid reason, they don't pass go and collect $200.

The answer to the question needs to be compelling because there will be days where your phone feels like it's 100 pounds and the last thing you want to do is pick it up and make another call. Or you'll dread breaking that uncomfortable silence and asking for the sale.

For example, saying that you want to earn more money may sound like an easy answer, but it's not enough. Money is great, but it's the "why" behind this money that's going to motivate you. Saying that you want to earn more money so you can move to a nicer neighborhood and send your kids to a better school is a "why" that will get you out of bed!

What's my why? Because, if we met, I hope you'd ask me.

Easy. It's the greatest job in the world—I'm in control of my income and I'm able to provide people with products and services that make a difference. Sales is the lifeblood of every organization, keeping organizations alive and payrolls met. Sales mean winning and getting paid for results. Sales mean education, integrity, and delivering value. And for me, as a young boy growing up with parents who owned a small business for over 30 years, sales meant gifts at Christmas, tuition to my Catholic school, basketball shoes, and family vacations with my three sisters. Sales are the reason many of my childhood memories exist. Thanks to the example of my parents, and the generations of entrepreneurs that came before them in my lineage, I understand that sales is the greatest job in the world. And it's the reason I'm passionate about helping salespeople and companies get better and sell more. It's personal. Sales isn't fluffy to me. It's the lifeblood of families, organizations, and communities.

## CHAPTER 3

# THE NEW STANDARDS OF SALES

The old way of selling is dead.

It died with the annoying and impersonal cold call. The rotary phone and the pushy salesperson, no thanks. It died when salespeople across the nation thought that they could manipulate and pressure prospects into buying. It slipped away when the emphasis was on corny techniques, instead of delivering value. It died when salespeople thought that email, text messaging, Facebook profiles, LinkedIn accounts, or Instagram were just fads. It passed quietly in the night when salespeople decided to use mind-numbing sales jargon instead of talking like real people.

These "salespeople" that adhere to the old way of selling deserve to be replaced. You've probably experienced one form of the "old way of selling" before. For me, recently, it was when I went to purchase a new vehicle. The salesperson smelled blood in the water and used every trick and tactic in the book to make sure that I took the car home *today*! This person tried microcommitments, boxing me in a corner, standing in my way as I decided to leave, and more. I was frustrated and frankly irritated by the hyper-aggressive approach, as most buyers would be. Make no mistake, these "salespeople" will be replaced. But, leaders, sales teams, and companies who understand this change will be rewarded. The sales revolution is happening and it's happening quicker than anyone realized.

Listen, people hate to be sold. It's a universal rule that (even if you're in sales) chances are you hate being sold. Even if you're good at sales (and since you're reading this book, you're most likely better than average) you still hate to be sold.

That's because crappy salespeople have given you and me a bad rap. Cheesy smiles, buzzwords, and pushy tactics leave a bad taste in our mouths.

So if everyone hates to be sold, why do salespeople still choose tricks instead of being authentic and personal? It baffles me when salespeople choose kitschy closing techniques instead of delivering a solution to someone's problem.

Enter...the *new* standards of sales, developed because I saw too many good people get into sales without any clue about how to have success in the game. I am grateful because I've had mentors who taught me the ropes, but I realize many people have bad mentors, received bad advice, or were left to figure it out on their own.

I'll share the Standards with you, but you have to promise me one thing. You're here because you actually want to raise your standards. You're tired of the status quo and want more from life and your career. If so, we're good. If not, don't waste your time or mine.

Here is the structure:

**Standard 1: Mindset**—Ten beliefs crucial to the foundation for success.

**Standard 2: Prep Work**—Framework and preparation that makes selling easy.

**Standard 3: Selling**—The Playbook, Sales Method and People Types that are the engine of Seven Figure Sales.

**Standard 4: Follow-Up**—Creative, consistent, and planned follow-up—the ultimate differentiator.

One more thing before we dive in. These Standards only work if you do. If you were expecting a get-rich-quick formula, I ask that you stop right here. This book is more than theory or techniques to memorize for the test, only to forget the lesson hours later. You need to put these thoughts into action every single day. Some days will be easier than others, but I guarantee they'll only work if you actually do the work. So *do* the work.

STANDARD 1: MINDSET

Every morning my wife takes our girls, Nina and Mae, to school and asks them the same three questions. Why? To get them in the right mindset for their day and to instill in them our family values. The questions and answers sound like this: (1) What's the most important decision you make every day? Our attitudes! (2) What do you know more than anything in the world? Mommy and Daddy love us more than anything, no matter what. (3) What do we believe in? We are strong, kind, and grateful!

Every day they say these same things because repetition is key. And through repetition, a positive mindset is reinforced.

So first things first, get your mind right. It takes work and repetition. But, regardless of your current position or salary, there is one common denominator of sales success—having the right mentality. The right mindset not only will set you apart from everyone else but will supercharge your success. Read *Standard 1: Mindset* and then reread it again in a few weeks until these lessons become second nature.

Imagine you were snowshoeing in the Grand Teton National Park in beautiful Wyoming. You're tired from a long day of hiking, covered in sweat and cold to the bone from the freezing temperatures. The sun is going down quickly, and you know that you have to get warm or you could become a human-flavored Popsicle for a bear. Now that you have to build a fire, you start scavenging for wood. You find three large trunk-sized pieces of pine that you have to muscle off of the ground and trudge through the snow to bring back to camp. It's a hard and arduous process, but you know that if you want a fire, you need wood. You try to light the large logs on fire with your flint and tinder, but for some reason, these large logs don't want to ignite. The sun has now fully gone down and it's starting to get dark and cold. You think, "this never happened to Bear Grylls," as you feverishly strike your flint over and over trying to get the big logs to light.

This is like the old way of selling. Many thought that to be successful, all they had to do was find some wood, light a match and voila, a fire! So many salespeople I've worked with try in vain for years thinking that it's the match's fault, so they strike harder, faster, and with more vigor.

Now take that same scenario but instead of lumbering through the woods with large pieces of wood, imagine focusing on small twigs, leaves, and branches to create the foundation of proper kindling. You find plenty of it, and so with little effort, you're able to start a fire. As you nurse that small fire, soon enough you feel the warmth on your face, hands, and feet. Your spirits lift and you start to prepare a warm dinner. You survive to hike another day!

Many people I've worked with don't realize that to start their own internal fire, they need to focus on building the right environment for a fire to flourish. They overlook the collection of little pieces of tinder, branches, and twigs necessary to really get a fire ready to light because they want to get straight to the part where they see a towering inferno.

Kindling is your mindset and your view on sales, success, and money. The mindset is the master key and the foundation for all sustainable sales and personal success.

### Mindset Standards:

1. Discipline Will Set You Free
2. Focus on Results, Not Methods
3. "Urgent" vs. Important
4. Keeping Score
5. You be You
6. Be Enthusiastic
7. Sales is a Grind
8. Iron Sharpens Iron
9. You Get Out What You Put In
10. Believe in Abundance

## CHAPTER 4

# DISCIPLINE WILL SET YOU FREE

For the majority of salespeople, discipline is a dirty word. They think discipline will hurt their mojo, impact their special sauce, or kill their creativity. Or for most salespeople with short attention spans, discipline is simply scary.

Why? Because most salespeople think discipline means the *lack* of freedom—freedom to be creative, to be themselves, or to be free to do as they please.

I'd argue the exact opposite. Discipline *leads* to freedom. Discipline actually *is* the key to sales success.

This idea isn't new. Jocko Willink goes deep into this concept in his book *Discipline Equals Freedom*, but I love to apply it to sales.

Growing up, to say I was undisciplined was an understatement. I procrastinated and avoided the hard work I knew I needed to do, so I found other activities to fill my time. That all changed on September 12, 2010, in beautiful Madison, Wisconsin while watching an Ironman competition.

An Ironman is one of the toughest endurance races. Competitors complete a 2.4-mile swim, 112-mile bike ride, and 26.2-mile run. As the saying goes, "Swim 2.4 miles! Bike 112 miles! Run 26.2 miles! Brag for the rest of your life!"

Hearing the sounds of the crowd and feeling the quiet determination of the competitors (including two family members!) slog away mile after mile had me instantly hooked. As we left that evening, I was hooked. I knew that I wanted to become an Ironman, but wanting to and becoming one were two very different things.

Anyone who signs up for an event like this needs to be committed. No one signs up and two months later competes. Training takes planning and at least two years of work. There were plenty of distractions going on at that time in my life because our oldest, Nina, was less than a year old and my wife was finishing up her master's degree.

But, I was committed and registered to compete in the Ironman. I started by getting a plan and setting up a system of accountability. Each day was easy because all I had to do was the workout that was prescribed for me by my coach (my wife's cousin, Lauren, a two-time Ironman World Championship finisher). If it was on the plan, I did the workout. Day in and day out for two years. There were *a lot* of days I didn't want to run, bike or swim. Training in Wisconsin ensured that I ran in the snow and in the dark for many months at a time. But, regardless of the weather, my mood, my infant daughter, or the circumstances around me, I did the work.

I crossed the finish line two years later in 13 hours and 25 minutes. During that day, while many of my fellow competitors struggled with nerves, I was quietly confident. I was confident in my training and confident that I had been disciplined to do the hard things that would make this race a success. I became a convert to discipline that day. I realized that the same level of discipline that can turn a newbie into an Ironman could turn the meekest of newbie salespeople into sales stars.

**If you want to be successful in sales, you need to embrace discipline.**

Discipline increases your knowledge and skills.
Discipline gives you momentum.
Discipline allows you to make more calls.

Discipline allows you to have better calls.

Discipline allows you to book more appointments.

Discipline leads to more closed deals.

Discipline leads to more commission.

Discipline leads to more vacations.

Discipline leads to better vacations.

Discipline makes your relationships better.

Discipline keeps you in shape.

Sounds nice, right? But then, why doesn't everyone do this?

**Salespeople commonly don't do the hard things it takes to make sales easy.**

And what's the hard thing? Discipline.

Discipline in who you target. Discipline in your daily activities, and weekly schedule, and doing what you say you'll do.

It's no different than the discipline elite athletes have to muster every day to stay at their absolute peak performance. Sure, we see pro football players take the field on Sunday, but we don't see the disciplined choices throughout the week and their entire career to get to that point.

While you may not be playing in front of thousands of fans every week, you do need to demonstrate a high degree of discipline. And since there aren't thousands of fans cheering you on, that discipline is something that you need to find every day. Day in and day out even when it's cold and February and you haven't seen the sun in three weeks. Or when it's summer, or the week of Christmas, or the Fourth of July.

**Discipline will set you free.**

Free to buy the watch you want.
Free to buy the car you want.
Free to work from wherever.
Free to get a personal trainer.
Free to take amazing vacations.
Free to create memorable experiences.
Free to realize your dreams.

It's worth it. I promise. Just program your mind to remember to raise your standard that discipline sets you free.

## CHAPTER 5

# FOCUS ON RESULTS, NOT METHODS

On Thanksgiving 2015, my former boss and mentor, Pete, was diagnosed with Stage IV Liver Cancer. He was a man who loved traveling the open road on his Harley, fishing on Little Cedar Lake, and smoking a cigar. He also loved messing with people, personal development, and soaking up all the moments that made life meaningful. He was a man of grit and character and tough love. That tough love carried through to me, and he instilled in me lessons about success that I think of every single day.

I tell you about Pete because when I'm lazy, unfocused, or unmotivated, I think of him and his consistent reminders to embrace the grind, hustle, and fantastic opportunities life can bring. Like he always said, "Go Make Action Happen."

Pete lost his battle with cancer in January 2017, but he never stopped fighting. Fighting for life and love and somewhat ironically, results. He wanted results with his treatment, and he drilled it in my head from day one that results are the only option at work too.

According to Pete, there are only two forms of activity—results-driven activity and methods-driven activity. He was never subtle about this, and he didn't sugar coat it. The more I think back about it, he was tough as hell on me.

But, this simple concept changed my daily focus, income, life, and career more than anything else I learned from him. I thought I was really hot shit in my early selling days, so he had to pound this concept into my head for months until I finally caught on.

The concept is this...salespeople either focus on results-driven activity or methods-driven activity.

**Methods-driven activity is the *illusion* of real productivity or getting results.**

**Results-driven activity is getting *results*...plain and simple.**

That's why sales is the greatest career in the world (in my opinion) because we keep score. You either close the deal or someone else wins. You get the commission or someone else does. Results-driven activity is the essential grind of sales, it's the part that most people don't want to do, and it's the difference between cashing checks or going hungry.

You can tell if someone is results or methods focused based on which category they fall into:

- 5 percent—The Achiever (people who are results focused!)
- 25 percent—The Wannabe Achiever (people who *wish* they were results focused!)
- 70 percent—The Job Seeker (people comfortable being methods driven!)

Achievers only make up 5 percent. They're the group that will consistently focus on results-driven activity. This is a rare breed indeed, and if you're one of them, I salute you. If you have one of them working for you, do whatever it takes to keep them at your company. They're über-focused, and won't let anyone get in the way of their results. While everyone else is usually taking a day off during March Madness, updating their fantasy football team, or cutting out early on Fridays, these rare breeds are still getting after it. They're the top performers, always in the President's Club and driving nice cars. Half the office usually despises them, yet they are responsible for making enough revenue to keep the lights on in the business and to keep the support staff paid. They speak in terms of results, not platitudes. They don't make excuses because they get it done. They don't complain about the compensation plan because they're usually maxing it out. These people could go into just about any industry and be successful. They understand that sales is a simple process. Do the right amount of results-driven activity for a consistent amount of time and you'll achieve success.

Wannabe Achievers represent 25 percent of people. They focus on results-driven activity only part of the time. Maybe they are not hungry enough, or perhaps they don't know what they're capable of, but either way, they're cheating themselves. They cheat themselves because they know what focusing on results-driven activity looks like, but they don't commit long term. They may have streaks of focus, but overall they drift in and out. They lack the courage to play at a high level day in and day out. They get distracted by new projects that only serve as a diversion.

Job Seekers make up the other 70 percent, or the majority of the world's salesforce. They're a lot of talk but little action. They talk about how busy they are but don't ever get the job done, close the big deal, or make the sale. Why? They spend the majority of their time in methods-driven activity.

Methods-driven activity looks a lot like preparing to do business, "prospect research," going to appointments that are non-value add, and checking email every one and a half minutes. It's an illusion of busyness, making it look like you are neck-deep in work, surrounded by the whirling dervish of perceived action. However, it's a house of cards. You put on a good show, but every Sunday night there's a gnawing pit in your stomach. You may know that feeling. You're wondering when you'll hit the sales lottery. You know that you won't make your goals, and you pray like hell that your boss won't take notice and start asking you the hard questions. This 70 percent of people are, sadly, methods-focused.

On the other hand, results-driven activity and working hard feels fantastic. Maybe it's only happened for a day, an afternoon or even an hour or two, but I know you've felt it. You concentrated on closing deals, you made more calls than ever, and you were dialed in. You even forgot to eat lunch because you were kicking ass and taking names. In the zone, in the flow, whatever you call it, you were focused on your results!

So don't settle or give in. It will be hard. It will not be easy. You will doubt yourself. You will challenge your ability to focus on results. You will think that you can't do this.

Believe me. Doing the hard things that will force you to focus on results will make you a better person. These difficult moments will define your career, life, and success. It's not easy, but being mediocre and broke isn't fun either.

Force yourself to concentrate on results-driven activity every day for as long as you can (remember, discipline will set you free). Find an accountability partner, get focused and hang a poster on your wall that asks..."Are you focused on results or methods right now?"

Thanks for helping raise my standards, Pete.

CHAPTER 6

# "URGENT" VS. IMPORTANT

It's easy to spend an entire day pinballing from putting out one fire only to go onto the next. You are "busy," but nothing gets done at the end of the day. If your day looks like this, you are focusing on *urgent* tasks.

You'll probably even be sure to tell me, "Ugh, I have so much to do"...because you'd have the time to chat in between responding to emails that don't need responses, checking your sports teams, surfing LinkedIn for people you'll never call, tracking a package, and emailing prospects asking if their money is ready yet instead of actually adding value. No matter how much time you have, your day will be full. You work from your inbox, are reactionary, and keep thinking about the "darn dailies." Your day is full of supposedly "urgent" tasks, and it feels like you're the ball in a game of pinball.

Maybe you've been one of these pinball victims, or you've worked with one in the past. I've run into my fair share throughout the years, but few were worse than an individual I'll call "Fred." Fred had a classic case of the gimmies (I'm testing your *Berenstain Bears* knowledge). Fred wanted all of the success and he talked such a good game. He promised me and everyone else on the sales team that he was going to be the killer-biller, with his name on the top of the leaderboard. He had huge goals of bringing in millions in revenue, allowing him to cash big checks and buy whatever he wanted.

Fred made a lot of promises, but when it came to weekly and monthly reviews he was always in the back quartile of the pack. After two months of this, I started getting concerned that there was a more significant issue with our product, marketing, or sales channel, so I closely observed Fred for a couple of days. As I settled in with a coffee, ready to peel back the onion and find a problem with our sales processes, I found Fred as frantic as a Kardashian in front of the paparazzi. Fred couldn't help himself from getting distracted by anything, everyone and all the things!

He'd bounce between email, to talking with a coworker, to reading, to calling, back to attempting to finish that original email, all within 10 minutes. And that was if someone didn't stop over to talk about the latest football game. This guy was the epitome of focusing all of his time and energy into a daily pinball of tasks.

After only a few short hours of observing him, I pulled Fred aside and asked him how he thought his day was going. And while his answer may surprise you, it's the one I hear from underproducing, but "overly busy" reps all the time. Fred thought that he was getting all sorts of work done, and was being super productive, although he had a hard time coming up with more than five examples of what he had done and actually completed.

Fred needed to prioritize his tasks between **urgent** and **important.** I told him as much and we put together an action plan that had him limit his distractions, work environment, and interaction with his coworkers. Fred stuck to the plan and his results improved dramatically.

Fred's day isn't too dissimilar to thousands of salespeople out in the workforce today. Maybe you work with one, manage one, or you are that person? Instead of pinballing like Fred, imagine a day where you were calm and laser-focused on *important* tasks like strategy, connecting with your team, adding value to your prospects, calling your customers, and moving the needle effectively toward your desired results.

Stop doing the things wrong that you know are wrong. Chances are you're not as oblivious as Fred was to his lack of productivity, but maybe you are, or you can recognize it in others. You know that there are things that you do today and probably every day that you should stop right now. You know you should stop, but you can't, or you won't.

Where do you spend your time? You can't say you're working if you're in email. You can't say you're productive if you keep pinballing between tasks with no focus. Substitute this scattered approach with discipline. Discipline is the key to take you off the hamster wheel of distraction to being the master of your day.

Trust me, I get it. The distractions are real. But shocker... there will *always* be distractions! There will always be things taking you away from the big work you're supposed to be doing. Check out the chart for some examples of what's urgent vs. important. Then, self-assess to see where you spend the majority of your day. I've left you some places to enter your examples.

| "Urgent" Activity | Important Activity |
| --- | --- |
| Pinballing from task to task | Focused time outside of inbox |
| Personal emails | Have a designated time to check and respond to personal emails |
| LinkedIn or Social Media Scrolling | Creating and sharing content that will add value to your prospects and customers on social media |

| "Urgent" Activity | Important Activity |
| --- | --- |
| Researching clients you probably won't call | Research three criteria you need to know and record the info (so you don't have to re-research it) |
| Calling, checking in and asking if they have money to buy yet | Calling and progressing deals forward in creative, value-added ways |
| Randomly, haphazardly calling/emailing with no set schedule | Developing and sticking to a cadence |
| Getting lost clicking in your CRM with no plan to reach out | Strategically find top buyers and pursue them (take action) |

**I spend the majority of my day:**

This standard applies to business and personal life. Have you ever met someone that is always complaining that they don't have enough time in their day or that they're too busy to fill-in-the-blank? Yet, you know for a fact that person also spends three hours a night watching *Game of Thrones* or *The Bachelor*. You can't have it both ways.

You can't be too busy to take massive action in your life and be up-to-date on every season of all the shows. You have to determine what is important and what is urgent. Knowing who makes it to the rose ceremony is "urgent," but building a business, transforming your health, or spending quality time with your spouse or family is important.

## CHAPTER 7

# KEEPING SCORE

There's a well-known story about Charles M. Schwab, the steel magnate born in 1862. The story goes, shared in the unforgettable *How to Win Friends and Influence People*, that Schwab was visiting an underperforming mill where the leader had tried everything to motivate his mill to perform.

Schwab devised a simple plan. As the day shift was leaving, he asked one of the men how many heats they performed that day. The man answered "six," and Schwab chalked an enormous number six on the floor. The night crew came in and inquired what the six was all about. The next morning the six was replaced with a seven by the night shift. This battle escalated, and a once underperforming mill was now one of the top producing operations.

Schwab tapped into the power of keeping score. And you can too.

Like Peter Drucker famously says, "What gets measured, gets managed."

In the world of sales, there are no participation trophies. Second place goes out of business, and you can't cash an honorable mention check. There is only winning and losing.

So, keeping score is a mindset that must weave into the fabric of your sales career. It's effective regardless of team size, industry, or experience level, and is one of the most overlooked tools in sales.

You see, sales is one of the few jobs where people keep score. Most jobs leave you in the dark, wondering how you compare to your peers. How do you know if you're a good accountant? Can you compare yourself to your peers on a weekly and monthly basis with units of measure that everyone agrees upon? Sales doesn't have that problem. It is one of the few careers where no one blinks an eye at ranking salespeople, or for that matter telling people what their commission and pay is. Imagine another job doing that!

Many companies, salespeople, and managers will balk at the idea of keeping score when it comes to sales. They cite a variety of reasons, but in between the protests and the uncomfortable silence, we all know the truth. They're afraid of being found out. This is absolutely the wrong mindset.

But having a mindset where keeping score is valuable leaves no place for anyone to hide. Don't shy away from this level of exposure. Embrace it. The transparency allows you to be honest with yourself. Are you doing the work to achieve your goals?

Keeping score doesn't have to be tricky, complicated, or confusing. You don't need over-engineered software and complicated math formulas. Take a lesson from Mr. Schwab. He used chalk.

Start with deciding on three to five metrics that are most valuable to your organization. I recommend no more than five. Anything more and salespeople don't know where to concentrate.

I like to start with calls/outreaches, appointments set or demos, and won deals. You can always add more, but think about your sales process and the most critical metrics in your organization. Make sure these are "easy" numbers for you to pull so reporting and posting the numbers takes no more than a few minutes a week. Be consistent and never miss a day or week. You need consistency to see patterns and have a score that's 100 percent accurate.

Next, you'll want to display these daily, weekly, or monthly results. You can use your CRM, create an Excel document, use a whiteboard or poster paper. Don't overcomplicate it, and use what you can find. The key here is visibility. Make it so simple to see and comprehend that even someone off the street who has no idea what your company does could easily understand who's doing well and who's not.

If you're a manager or leader of a sales team, keeping score brings clarity to you as the leader and brings motivation to the sales team. In my experience, there are two types of individuals who compete in the sales world—those that compete against each other, and those that compete against themselves. Both are important and knowing who on your team is which type will help you manage their motivations and their scorecard.

For example, for those competing against themselves, the simple act of goal setting and rewards can do the trick. Establish a lofty goal and encourage them to associate a reward that's a splurge—something tangible they wouldn't usually spend money on. These seemingly simple tactics can have a considerable impact.

At a previous job, we implemented the mindset of keeping score, and it didn't take long for the CEO to pay close attention to the scorecard. He would congratulate the top performers and help coach up those at the bottom. The top performers loved it, and it motivated them to achieve at an even higher rate and compete amongst their peers. Many of them told me that it felt great to be pushed, and they appreciated the encouragement and congratulations from the CEO. They wanted to win, and they'd do whatever they could to be the top dog. Sales skyrocketed.

Not surprisingly, the performers consistently in the bottom hated it. Some of them would make radical changes and get out from the lower positions; others would complain about the scorecard. The latter half usually didn't stay too long. They didn't like the pressure, and always had a myriad of excuses at the ready.

Whether you're the leader of a sales team or an individual looking to increase their results, you can use this mindset to raise standards. It will be uncomfortable at first, and many will fight it like kids eating veggies at the dinner table. If you're an individual looking to hold yourself to this standard, there will be days when you don't want to do it. Press on. Don't give in and don't give up. Be patient and look for little wins. Start small and be consistent with publishing your scorecard. As Schwab demonstrated, it doesn't take fancy tools to be effective.

## CHAPTER 8

# YOU BE YOU

Many salespeople try to cookie-cutter copy other sales-people. They wear a shiny suit, have super white teeth, and act like Rico Suave. They become a smooth talker or assume they should live a life of golf, country clubs, and slicked-back hair.

You don't need to be that person. You don't need to compare yourself to the next sales guru. It's inauthentic. I'm here to tell you that you can be likable, and all you have to be is you. *You* are your greatest asset. I'm just a Midwestern dude who's been balding since he was nineteen, but I am comfortable in my skin, and that reflects in my confidence when I sell and talk to people.

**You be you.**

Salespeople just need to be themselves to be successful. You don't need to act or look like you know everything. Be vulnerable. Don't be afraid to say what you don't know. Let your guard down and let your buyers get to know the real you. A fake veneer of confidence won't get you very far. People gravitate toward genuine people (and sales reps) and they'll recognize your sincere attempts as just what they are—sincere efforts to make a connection more significant than a sales transaction. That connection is priceless.

I will get into this later, but it's imperative to understand that being your true self means that you'll have to maintain your uniqueness while also adapting to your prospect's personality (see Chapter 26 on People Types). For example, my mother-in-law used to sell real estate and called herself a "chameleon." She could genuinely connect with small-town farmers, clueless first-time home buyers, or people looking to invest in another seven-figure home. No matter, she adapted herself to make the individuals feel comfortable while also living up to her personality.

Similarly, I've had the awesome opportunity to lead a group of 50+ sales and service professionals that took inbound calls all day. They had to explain a somewhat complex insurance subscription-based membership. Yes, that's not a typo. The product we were selling was an insurance subscription membership. Trust me when I say that no one wakes up one day wanting to buy this product. It has to be sold.

After listening to countless calls, it became apparent. We were over complicating our product. We were asking our sales and service staff to be, act and sound like people that they weren't. So we introduced a new initiative that will seem unorthodox but worked with amazing results.

We coached our sales and service pros to explain and talk about the product as if they were having a beer with a friend at their local pub. They didn't need to pretend to be anything that they weren't. They simply had to speak at a level they'd feel comfortable with (minus any profanity and alcohol)! This dramatically improved our conversations, and our conversion and sales numbers took off like a rocket.

That story may seem counterintuitive, but when you know your audience, you can speak to your audience on their terms. This leads to an increased level of trust, and once they trust you, they'll buy from you.

One of the biggest pet peeves that I hear prospects, friends, family, and coworkers complain about is when salespeople pretend to know everything. Have you ever had the experience of working with a salesperson who is so eager to demonstrate all of their knowledge that they're trying to finish your sentence? I don't think there's anything more demeaning or annoying in a sales situation than when a salesperson thinks they have the prospect all figured out. It's even worse when the prospect knows the sales rep doesn't have the foggiest idea about their needs.

I have a newsflash. If you don't know the answer, say you don't know the answer! Don't feed me a line of bullshit and marshmallows and think I won't pick up on it. I will, and so will your prospect. It's a pretty widely accepted figure that 70 percent of buyers research your product and your competitors before they even pick up the phone. Today's buyer is smarter than ever, so don't lie.

Salespeople lie because they don't want to be seen as incompetent or dumb, but these two adjectives are far better than being known as a liar or a "slick salesman." Be confident in who you are and be confident enough to know that sometimes the best answer is a "let me get back to you on that." And just as important is getting back to them with the solution in a timely fashion.

So if you want to sell more, be your likable self. Don't try to be someone you're not. At the end of the day you're selling to a person, so act the part. You be you!

---

## CHAPTER 9

# BE ENTHUSIASTIC

There are two superpowers that if every person on this earth demonstrated in great generosity and quantity, this world would be a far better and different place.

The first superpower is **gratitude**. There are thousands of books on the topic, but it's very simple and *so* important... be grateful. Gratitude goes a *long* way. At work, at home, with friends, with family, in your world, and in your soul.

The second superpower is great for life, but is über-essential for anyone pursuing a career in sales. It's the superpower of **enthusiasm**!

How do I define enthusiasm? It's not as easy to explain with words. So, let me paraphrase Justice Potter Stewart's famous thoughts on pornography—"I can't define it, but I know it when I see it." Boom, that's a classic line right there.

Enthusiasm isn't something that you define. It's something that you feel and know when you see it. I know when I'm enthusiastic and when I'm not, and I'm guessing you do too.

When it comes to sales, have you ever been pitched by someone who is Johnny Raincloud or Sally Wet Blanket? They're just a total wet noodle with zero enthusiasm for their company, their product, or even the great career of sales? How enthused were you to pull out your wallet and buy their product? I'm guessing that even if you did choose to purchase something from them, it was either because you felt bad for them or they were the only game in town.

I believe that there is a direct correlation between sales success and enthusiasm. Today's buyer of any widget, service, or product has thousands of options that they can access at any time and anywhere. Enthusiasm gives sales pros a competitive advantage, and can be the difference between the President's Club or complaining about your nonexistent commission check. Enthusiasm acts as a lightning rod for your personal brand, and people buy from people they like.

I first learned this in the competitive world of recruiting and staffing. I figured out that if I demonstrated a level of enthusiasm that was genuine, I could get the person sitting across the table from me energized about what I was selling. Whether it was selling a company a consulting engagement or convincing an engineer to take a new job, the more enthusiastic I got, the more likely I was to close the deal. And trust me, some of these engineers didn't get enthusiastic for much. Maybe you know the type.

People may say that they buy off logic, but people shop on logic and buy on emotion. Sure, you may shop for a nice new truck because your current one is rusting out (logic), but you bought that truck for its impressive sound system, big tires, and because it's nicer than your neighbor's (emotion). Enthusiasm creates an emotional tie, and that tie, when used right, can take you to the top of any selling organization.

Whenever I'm having a hard day, one of the easiest cures I know is to demonstrate enthusiasm. You probably thought I was going to say "drink Scotch"...not so fast! It sounds simplistic, and that's because it is. Whenever I have a day where my energy is drained, and I honestly don't want to deal with people, I've found that the most straightforward path out of that mindset is to be enthusiastic to whomever I'm around.

I do this because enthusiasm begets enthusiasm. If I get enthusiastic, I know there's a damn good chance that the person I'm speaking with will become excited about my ideas and *me*! That's the little spark that if I nurture right can turn into a raging inferno, thanks to the gasoline of enthusiasm.

The reason for this is the Law of Reciprocity. When someone does something nice for you or treats you nicely, you are hardwired psychologically to do something nice in return. In my experience with enthusiasm, some people respond even more positively than my original enthusiastic nature.

It's science.

So think about this. I can completely change my surroundings to always cater to having people be enthusiastic toward me and my ideas just by being enthusiastic.

This world is tough enough as it is, especially for the typical person trying to make a career in sales. You've got numbers to hit and bosses to satisfy. Or, maybe you're a sales leader or the entrepreneur of the organization, and the stresses and opportunities come at you from all directions.

Being a selling organization can be an uphill grind. But, regardless of what's going on in your life, you can still be enthusiastic. It's free, I checked.

Enthusiasm makes people feel awesome, and why not leave them with the feeling of awesome? Awesome is fun, and fun wins. Enthusiasm will help you be memorable and stand out from the crowd. Don't underestimate it.

Brian Tracy is known for stating that sales is the transfer of enthusiasm—transferring the raw energy from your mind and body about your product to the purchaser.

One of the easiest ways to do this is to simply be enthusiastic about your company, product, and mission in life.

When I first started out in sales, I had to be enthusiastic. In the early part of my career, it was one of the only reasons people bought from me. Honestly, it was. I asked them! And the response was commonly, "I bought from you because you seemed so darn excited about what you were selling!" Cha-ching! Once I got better at selling I didn't abandon my enthusiastic nature, I doubled down and reaped the results and the rewards.

## The Enthusiasm Challenge

Try this! Take the Enthusiasm Challenge. Over the next week, be as enthusiastic as you can in all areas of your life—with your family, friends, spouse, kids, and colleagues...even the waiter or waitress when you're next out to lunch or dinner. Remember their name when they introduce themselves, say please and thank you, ask them about their day and genuinely care. You'll get way better service and won't question if they've sneezed in your food.

Dive feet first into your selling career and demonstrate this new zeal for life to your clients and prospects. If you show up with anything less, start over. Be enthusiastic until it becomes a habit and then just a part of your character.

I can guarantee that your quality of life and work will improve. I hope you see the results I do and will take to making enthusiasm your superpower. Wouldn't you rather be known for being too enthusiastic than not being remembered at all? I would.

# CHAPTER 10

# SALES IS A GRIND

If you asked me what I wanted to be when I was fifteen years old, my answer was to be in sales. I'm still proud of that answer, but here's why I *thought* I wanted to be in sales.

I thought I'd get a company car, free cell phone (ahem, Motorola Razr anyone?!) and play golf every day. Yup, that's what I thought sales was all about...golf, schmoozing, cars, dinners out. Fun days followed by easy peasy signatures on the dotted line. No work, just fun.

But let's get real. If you've been in sales for more than one day, you know that it's far from that.

Sales is a grind because sales take energy and we actually keep score. You either made the calls or you didn't. You either got the contract signed or you didn't. Pretty simple, right?

You have to do the dirty work like meeting with people that don't want to give you the time of day, call people that don't call you back, work with people that don't want to work with you! And to succeed in sales, you need to do more of this work than everyone else.

A former boss and mentor of mine who's a super successful entrepreneur has a great saying. "Opportunity often looks a lot like hard work," he said paraphrasing Thomas Edison. I loved this from the day I heard it, and deep down I know this was meant for sales.

So go ahead. Make the calls you said you would make, meet the people you said you would meet, and do the difficult things you know that will make you a success, and don't stop.

Also, let me be very clear about something. I'm not talking about "trying" to do the work necessary to be successful in sales. I'm talking about *actually* doing the work.

So many people trade in the currency of "try" that it might as well be their calling card. They might as well deal exclusively in "tries" which makes it one of the world's most abundant commodities with no value.

You tried to make those calls, but got distracted.

You tried to set an appointment, but the prospect wasn't interested in your pitch.

You tried to close the deal, but they want to shop around.

Try, try, try. It doesn't matter, don't care, show me the results. Bill Parcells, arguably one of the toughest coaches in the NFL since Vince Lombardi, had a great saying, "Don't tell me about the pain, show me the baby."

Start *doing*! At the end of the day, your prospects, customers, boss, family, and paycheck are not interested in how hard you "try." They're only interested in how well you do. You can't deposit trying!

Don't blame it on the market, the economy, the industry, the president, the timing, the holiday season, the weather, the commission plan, or the boss.

Just stop.

Regardless of what bullshit story you're trying to convince yourself of today, let them go. Let them *all* go. These excuses won't do anything for you. They won't help you achieve the results you're looking for nor will they cash any checks for you.

As Jordan Belfort (yes, that guy from *The Wolf of Wall Street*) says, "The only thing standing between you and your goal is the bullshit story you keep telling yourself as to why you can't achieve it."

One last thing about why sales is a grind.

Sales is a blue-collar job dressed up as a white-collar job.

You read that right.

**Sales is just a good ol' blue-collar job dressed up as a white-collar job.**

It looks lighthearted, maybe even easy breezy. But as you'll see, sales requires the discipline of a West Virginian coal miner. Punch in and punch out, day in and day out. Sometimes you won't see the sun. Sometimes you'll feel like you're in the dark swinging your pickax into the unknown just hoping to make contact, wondering when or if you will ever strike gold.

Don't let the fancy clothes, cars, and potential fool you. No one trips out of the car and makes six figures unless you're the boss's kid. It takes a concerted effort day after day, month after month. But don't give up.

There will be plenty of your coworkers and competitors who will take the leisurely road of sales, but not you. By the sheer fact that you picked up this book and you read this far tells me that I'm telling you something you don't already know. So embrace the work. Enjoy the grind. Earn your weekend. And as I say to my team, TGIF. The Grind Includes Friday. Go get after it.

## CHAPTER 11

# IRON SHARPENS IRON

Personal development is a lot like an all-you-can-eat buffet. Some people go hungry, some only get one helping, and others go back for fourths. Be the person that goes back for fourths. I don't believe in starving for personal development. The only thing standing in your way between the success you want to become and where you are today is how aggressive you are in attaining that knowledge. So, fill up your plate.

*As iron sharpens iron, so one person sharpens another.*
—Proverbs 27:17

To me, this statement means that to professionally and personally grow, I need to be around people that force me to become better. It means putting myself in situations that challenge me to struggle and grow, to become a better husband, father, leader, and salesperson.

Every time I read that verse, I feel quiet pride that stirs deep in my soul. It's as accurate now as it was thousands of years ago when it was first recorded. I believe in this statement so much that my wife gifted me a silver paperweight with this inscription a few years back.

Here are three strategies that you can use to personally and professionally grow and "sharpen your iron."

First, in my experience (regardless of career path) the individuals who are succeeding have one major advantage. They had a mentor. They had someone at an early point in their career who invested a lot of time, effort, and dedication into giving that individual honest—and I'm sure at times challenging—feedback.

I cannot stress enough the importance of having a mentor. This is how, over time, people I look up to became the big cheese, the killer biller, the decision-maker, or the person stealing all of your business.

I've had the incredible opportunity to learn and heed advice from some great mentors. I don't know why they share time and advice with me, but I'm damn thankful for the many who have been a mentor to me. I can tell you without a shred of doubt that I could not live the life I have now if it weren't for these people and their words and advice. Special thanks to my Mom, Dad, John, Sam, Tim G, Pete, Bruce and Donna, Tim S, Brad, Chris, and so many others.

If you have a mentor now, continue to let that individual challenge you, and give you as honest feedback as allowed by the laws that govern your state. If you don't have a mentor, change jobs, cities, or states. There are even hundreds of online resources and groups that can act as your virtual mentor. So really, there's no excuse. You just have to put yourself out there.

Once you've found your mentor, here's what I recommend. Begin by asking them for advice. Start small and build a foundation and a relationship. Next, report back on that advice. Did you use it? What benefits did you get? What pitfalls did you encounter? Don't waste the opportunity to throw a little thanks and gratitude their way. Most people love to dispense their knowledge or advice, so ask for it and say thank you for it. If having a mentor at work isn't an option, find someone that you connect with on LinkedIn, that went to your college, or high school. Hell, if you can't find anyone, I'll help you out, but be prepared to work hard and be challenged.

Mentors don't even have to be personal connections or contacts. We live in an incredible time! Not only can you watch or listen to hundreds of hours of content from some of the best motivators and speakers that ever existed, you can also get an insight into what some of the most successful people do every day with social media. Just think about it. Before social media, your ability to know what a leader like Richard Branson thought was limited to TV interviews and his books. Now you can watch YouTube or listen to a few podcasts to get insights into how he thinks and works.

Finding and utilizing a mentor in "real life" doesn't have to be a formal process. There doesn't have to be an exchange of secret handshakes or code words. It can be as informal as you like. Your mentor doesn't even have to know that they are "officially" your mentor! Skip the pomp and circumstance for honest questions, taking action, and reporting back on how their advice helped.

Also, get ready to make mistakes in front of your mentor. You have to be vulnerable and not be afraid to fail in front of this person. Take them behind the scenes. Don't just let them in on the successes, show them failures. That's where you're going to get the most out of this.

They might give you very honest and very candid feedback. When your mentor bestows upon you this feedback, be quiet and absorb. Don't make excuses. Feedback is a gift, and treat it as the honor it is. Be grateful that they care that much about you to invest their time into your success.

Remember that what separates you from where you want to be is the experience and knowledge it takes to walk that path. By putting yourself out there, and with the direction and help of a mentor, you will get there. And along your way, don't forget to look back and be a mentor to the next person in line.

Second, I need to channel one of my favorite mentors. I never got the chance to meet him, but his spirit lives on in print—Mr. Jim Rohn! I think he said it best, "You are the average of the five people you spend the most time with."

So, who are you spending your time with?

What does your choice of friends say about you?

Are they helping you grow, or are they an anchor in your pursuit?

Most likely, the five people you spend the most time with are family, coworkers, and friends. Make sure that you're spending your time wisely. So many people are held back by the negative associations that they have in their lives. Remember that you are responsible for who you spend time with.

You deserve to be around people who support you, strengthen you, and push you beyond your perceived limits. Don't hesitate to remove those that are holding you back so you're able to spend time with those who will force you to grow. This will not be easy.

If you have negative family members, distance yourself.

If you have negative friends, avoid them.

If you have negative coworkers, perhaps find a new job.

This may sound extreme, but Jim was right. You become the average of the people you most frequently associate with, so make sure it's a kick-ass five people.

Lastly, be aggressive in your pursuit of knowledge. This is only one of the thousands of books written on the topic of sales, personal development, and attitude. Don't let the books go unread. Don't let podcasts go unlistened to and don't let the seminar go unattended.

If you're going to be serious about dramatically improving your life, don't waste time by not developing your knowledge and skills. So many people I've worked with in the past have time for three hours of television a night, but complain that they don't have enough time to read a book. Don't be that person. Don't go hungry in your pursuit of knowledge. Don't starve yourself of ideas that could improve your life and the lives of your family. You're not a finished product.

"You will be the same person in five years as you are today except for the people you meet and the books you read," encourages the legendary Charlie "Tremendous" Jones. *So* true.

A great entrepreneur and mentor of mine taught me that there is always something to learn. One of his core values is that people and businesses are either growing or dying. Pretty awesome, right?! The top performers are students of the game. They're always in a beginner's mindset hunting for the latest piece of knowledge that they can capture, learn, and implement. Don't be too proud to think that you can't improve.

Don't starve yourself of this vital life lesson. It won't be easy, because watching Netflix will be way easier, but it won't get you to your goals. It won't get you to lead the life and career you were made for and deeply desire.

Here are my top ten books:

1. *Think and Grow Rich*, Napoleon Hill
2. *Strangest Secret*, Earl Nightingale
3. *It's Not How Good You Are, It's How Good You Want to Be*, Paul Arden
4. *Little Gold Book of YES! Attitude*, Jeffrey Gitomer
5. *Bunkhouse Logic*, Ben Stein
6. *Extreme Ownership*, Jocko Willink
7. *The Alchemist*, Paulo Coelho

8. *Twelve Pillars of Success*, Jim Rohn
9. *How to Win Friends and Influence People*, Dale Carnegie
10. Any of Ian Fleming's James Bond books!

**Books**

What books motivate you? Write them here so you can get reading or rereading.

# CHAPTER 12

---

# YOU GET OUT WHAT YOU PUT IN

One of the greatest things about choosing a career in sales is the clarity it brings to performance. In a highly visible team, it's easy to see who the winners and who the losers are. That's one of the main reasons why sales isn't for everyone.

Sales operates off of a pretty obvious scorecard as we talked about in Chapter 7: Keeping Score. Did you make the sale, or did you fail? That's it. Sales is as caveman as it gets. You either clubbed the woolly mammoth and feast, or you go hungry in your cave. The modern version of this is six-figure plus earnings and a crushed quota or living off your base.

As the old saying goes, your actions speak louder than words. In sales, those actions are the tell-all of success—making the extra call or cutting out early on a Friday, sticking to your schedule or scrolling through social media for an hour. These are the actions that will either lead you to the promised land or out to look for the next lousy job. Remember, discipline will set you free...especially when you dial into results-driving activity.

So, are your actions in line with your goals? Start by taking at least an hour to work through these next two activities—the Dreamboard and the Big Five. Pour yourself a drink (bourbon, coffee, tea, beet juice, your choice) and get ready to go deep.

You can get as creative as you'd like, but I recommend trying to keep it super simple.

### Dreamboard

We'll start with your Dreamboard. Take a standard issue 8.5x11-inch piece of paper. Draw one line down the middle horizontally, and one line down the middle vertically. You should have four equal boxes. Next, write each title in a separate box. Then, read the prompts to fill each box.

WANT

DO

GIVE

GROW

- **WANT**—What objects/things do you want? This is always a fun one. New car anyone? How about a fancy-schmancy Rolex, designer handbag, or a vacation home on the lake? The point is to start with objects because most people associate nice things with success. Nice things should not be your only focus, but having awesome things is a lot better than having crappy things.

- **DO**—What do you want to do and experience? Experiences usually consist of vacations and lifestyle. Heading to South Africa for a safari or sipping a mai tai at an exclusive resort with your family? It could be wine tastings in Napa or Bordeaux. For sports fans, it might be attending the Masters or following your alma mater to the Final Four. No matter what your ultimate experiences are, make sure they're vivid.

- **GIVE**—How do you want to give back to your community? What contributions to the world will you make? My wife and I give lots of our time, talent, and treasure to our community nonprofits. It's often hard work with little recognition, but honestly, it's some of the most important work we do. I'm a firm believer that you get back what you give 100 times over. And as my wife says over and over, "To whom much is given, much is expected" (Luke 12:48). If you don't volunteer or give to those who need it, start today. As Joe Polish says, "People who say money can't buy happiness haven't given enough away." You don't have to start your own trust or scholarship fund to make a real difference. Remember, simple acts go a long way.

- **GROW**—How do you want to improve yourself? People and businesses are either growing or dying. How will you improve your skills and personal development this year? Who will you surround yourself with? Will you join a mastermind, get a mentor, or focus on developing fundamental skills? Don't hold yourself back.

When applicable, use pictures—from a magazine, Google, or Pinterest. Otherwise, keep it simple and write words or draw little sketches. It doesn't have to be pretty.

Make several copies of your Dreamboard and make sure it's in a spot that you'll see every single day. I have one at my desk, on my bathroom mirror, next to my watch, and even in my car. Treat your goals as if they were your cell phone, always within an arm's reach.

Besides being a daily motivational tool for yourself, use it if you manage others. For example, if I'm working with a new corporation, sales team, or individual sales pro, I always start with asking them to create a Dreamboard. Nothing gives me more insight or leverage than knowing real goals.

So for me, if I commit to a day's worth of activities and I don't get them done, I ask myself if what's on my Dreamboard is still important? If it is, I ask myself why I didn't do the activities necessary to achieve my goals? For example, I know scheduling five new appointments every week will help grow my business, allowing me to obtain what's on my Dreamboard. But for the past two weeks, I've been distracted by other activities. I'll pull out my Dreamboard and do a self-assessment. Is the level of activity I'm producing good enough for me to get what I want on my Dreamboard?

Same goes if you're a sales leader. Instead of saying, "why didn't you hit your numbers?" Calmly pull out their Dreamboard, ask them if what's on the Dreamboard is still important, and then ask if their activities will allow them to cross off their dreams like a grocery list...and then be quiet. Don't say another word until they do. The answer will tell you all you need to know. And you can provide a coaching opportunity no matter their answer.

If you or your team feel like you're doing everything you can, then it could be a knowledge gap. We can work with that.

If you or your team are not working up to the standard you set, then you need to readjust, realign, and start taking some action. Because remember, you get out what you put in. Raise your standards.

Whatever you put on your Dreamboard won't work unless you start working. The Dreamboard fairy will not come and magically make it a reality.

Sales isn't one of those programs where you can think about closing more deals and then like magic your phone will start ringing off the hook. You'll need actually to go out there and make it happen.

There is another method I use to make sure my mind is always focused on what I want—the Big Five.

I read a few years ago that the average human brain has anywhere from 50,000 to 70,000 separate thoughts per day. Your brain is overwhelmed and doesn't know where to focus. How could it with 70,000 thoughts per day? Everything is important, new, and needs attention! As someone who is as scatter-brained and distracted often, this is what I do.

### The Big Five

Get a stack of 3x5-inch index cards. Yes, cheap regular index cards. On the index cards place five simple words that summarize primary life goals. These words represent the five goals to devote time, effort, and energy into achieving at all costs. I call it the "Big Five." These can evolve and change over time as you accomplish your goals or priorities change, but they should be overarching intentions for significant things.

Repeat them over and over, and know them by heart. If you ever ask, I'm able to produce my index card on the spot. You could keep one in your wallet, purse, your car, at your desk or in your gym bag. Just keep it around.

**BIG FIVE**

1.

2.

3.

4.

5.

I like it when my "Big Five" are memorable phrases or numbers that are meaningful. Here are some I've used over the years:

- 140.6—The number I was after when training for an Ironman, representing the number of total miles in the triathlon.
- 25—The number of books I want to read in a year.
- Clean—How I like to eat.
- Present and Fun—How I want to be as a father to my daughters.
- Enthusiasm—Because you can never be too enthusiastic.

- Write—Putting in the work of writing a book required the constant reminder to simply write.
- Energy—The reminder to be conscious of the energy I bring into a space.

If we met and I asked you to produce your goals, could you summarize your most important work into just five words on one 3x5 index card? If you can't, and can't possibly fathom boiling all you want down to only five points, imagine how hard it is for your brain to distinguish between the "urgent" and the important. Your brain has to know what you want most, so it knows how much energy to put in.

If you don't get anything else from this book, do yourself a favor, buy some plain old index cards and get busy. Get serious about this life, career, and the mark you want to make in the world. You deserve more. You deserve better.

Know what you want so that when you put in the work, you'll attain your dreams.

## CHAPTER 13

# BELIEVE IN ABUNDANCE

I'm convinced there are two types of people in this world. Jealous people who think one person's success means one less seat at the success table. And people who believe the success table is never-ending and can always fit more chairs.

The best people in sales believe the table is long and includes seats for everyone. They believe in abundance and shun scarcity. Scarcity means there's a finite amount of wealth, leads, prospects and customers. Have you ever seen little kids at the beach battle in toddler turf wars over the sand? Having a scarcity mindset is a lot like that. Imagine toddlers fighting over the privilege to scoop sand into a bucket. They're missing the fact that sand is everywhere and practically infinite!

I had the fortunate and unfortunate experience to see this firsthand. I worked for several years with an individual we'll call Brandon. He was a sales machine, and it didn't matter who or what was in his way—he was going for the win. Brandon hoarded clients and leads like he was Gollum from *Lord of the Rings* and any name was his "precious."

Brandon had more leads than one person could handle, and although he didn't intend to reach out to them, he refused to give them up to other reps. Sadly, this meant these leads were uncalled on because he was "too busy" while other reps were like koi fish waiting to jump on crumbs thrown into the pond. If Brandon embraced abundance, these untouched leads could have turned into clients, fueling more growth for the company.

Some people believe there is a set amount of channels from where leads originate. This scarcity mentality leads to "me, me, me" thinking—characterized by the mindset that there is only so much pie, and anytime you take a piece, that's one less piece for me. So these people hoard leads. They live in fear that someone else is going to take it, beat them, and they'll be gone forever. They lament, "That would've been a big account for *me*."

Just like sand at the beach, leads are infinite. The people you can call on are vast. There are more customers and opportunities than you can handle. So instead of focusing on protecting your territory or leads, focus on the abundance of opportunity, leads, relationships, and customers that exist.

This mindset creates an abundance of income, too. Win-win.

And, salespeople focused on providing value, sharing leads, being an advisor, being an educator, being helpful, and laying deep roots of relationships are way better off.

Every time the trap of scarcity and worry tempts you, say to yourself, "There's more where that came from!"

Don't hitch your wagon to one or two current customers. If you lose them to competition or timing or budget, say, "There's more where that came from!" A salesperson living up to their standards confidently knows that their healthy pipeline will carry them through.

Embrace an abundant mindset both in business and in your personal life. We only get a few precious years on this planet, so spending them with your fingers tightly wrapped (scarcity) only closes you off from some amazing possibilities (abundance).

STANDARD 2:

# PREP WORK

Have you ever had a new sales job where this happened? After a two- or three-day rundown of product and process, a day shadowing a more seasoned sales rep, and a tour of the building, your boss shows you to your desk, hands you a stack of old business cards and without much fanfare tells you to smile and dial. Great pep talk, coach! Well, lucky for you, in my world...this is the old way of selling.

The new way of selling is like the philosophy that originated in gourmet French cooking. *Mise en place* or "everything in its place"—the time when sauces are made, onions are chopped, and spices are measured. Chefs rely on this activity to maximize efficiency and to prepare for a busy night in the kitchen, ensuring the dishes that reach discerning diners are executed to perfection.

In sales, mise en place means prep work. Understanding the activities that lead to success and what your time should look like day by day, and hour by hour is crucial. Most salespeople bypass *mise en place* and want to get out there and start making things happen. Hold your horses, Mr. or Mrs. Antsy Pants. Your ducks need to be in a row first. Everything needs to be "in its place."

You only get one chance at a first impression, so it better be a damn good one. You might never get a second chance, so make sure you're on point. How? Prep work. *Mise en place.*

Because the best salespeople aren't lucky, they do prep work.

Standard 2: Prep Work cannot be overlooked. It's a non-negotiable. Commit and you'll already be ahead of your competition.

Most people don't work hard enough or smart enough to make sales easier, and prep work is just that. It's not sexy, but it's critical to sustained selling success.

## Prep Work Standards

- Funnel Math
- Ideal Day
- The Almighty Power Hour
- Know Thy Buyer
- Sink or Swim Test
- The Triangle Drill
- Your Best Social Self

---

## CHAPTER 14

# FUNNEL MATH

If you have a fully funded trust fund and are reading this book for entertainment, feel free to skip over this chapter. If you're hungry, motivated, and driven, this part is for you because in my yard money does *not* grow on trees.

Most salespeople want a nice new car and a big house, but don't know exactly how to get there. I know this feeling all too well. I used to think that my commission structure and the amount of activity I needed to do to get to my goals was like a secret code that I couldn't decipher.

That was until I learned how to do funnel math. Funnel math is a simple concept in sales where you can reverse engineer your goal and your daily activity plan. In other words, it's the activity you need to do to earn the money you want. I'm a visual individual who's very goal driven, and with a slight touch of ADD...like lots of salespeople. Once I was able to boil my day down from the mysterious ether of activity to a set number of *focused* activities, my career changed dramatically.

Getting clear on funnel math will also bring clarity and focus to your day, goals, and career. Once I was able to really understand funnel math, I didn't have to worry about all of the extraneous stuff I always stressed myself out about. I didn't have to worry about how the economy was doing or what my competition was doing. I just focused on my funnel math, adjusted when necessary, and plowed ahead toward my goal. Once I made this realization, it was liberating, and I know it will work for you.

Don't convince yourself that sales has to be this complex formula. Understand the activities you need to execute every day to move forward, do the activities, try to do them better than the day before, and you'll achieve all the results you desire.

The great part about understanding the math is that it's irrefutable. Let me warn you, though. Most people who go through funnel math prefer to live in a mushy cloud of bullshit. Sure, these salespeople talk big. They want to make well over a six-figure income, but as soon as I introduce them to the math and they compare the amount of activity and deals they need to close, they fold like a lawn chair.

To make your dreams a reality, you need to get very honest with yourself and what you're willing to do to achieve your goal. This doesn't mean to water down your dreams. Keep your goals large and in charge because now you'll finally have a path to achieve what you desire.

Remember the goals you have don't grow on trees. For you to achieve them, you'll have to battle day in and day out. Some days will be easier than others. Don't get distracted by the daily ups and downs. Instead, focus on continued progress toward a worthwhile goal.

Both successful salespeople and unsuccessful salespeople all dislike doing the hard things it takes to make sales easy and to be successful. The difference between the two is that the successful salesperson will still complete the things they dislike. The unsuccessful salesperson will skip them in favor of something easier.

Here's the math. Pretend I'm working with a new rep named Emma who wants to make $100,000/year and she gets a 5 percent commission on all sales on top of her $40,000 base. Emma's company's average sale is $25,000.

For each average sale of $25K, with a 5 percent commission, Emma will earn $1,250.

She wants to make $100K, which leaves $60K to earn in commission (on top of her $40K base).

So, to understand how many sales she'll need to make in the year, she takes $60K divided by $1,250. Emma will need to make 48 sales in the year, or about one a week.

| Salary Goal | $100,000 / year | $60,000 Needed in Commission to Reach Goal | $60,000 ÷ $1,250 |
|---|---|---|---|
| Current Base | $40,000 / year | | |
| Commission | 5% | $1,250 Commission on Average Sale | 48 Sales Needed |
| Average Sale Amount | $25,000 | | |

I encourage you to take it one step further and really examine how many calls will this take. How many demos need to be scheduled? Think about your input on these daily activities to get the annual output you want.

Use funnel math as a thermometer to keep track of your progress. This prep work provides needed clarity so that you always know where you are versus your big goals! Go get 'em.

| Salary Goal | $_____ | $_____ Goal − Current Base = A | A ÷ B |
|---|---|---|---|
| Current Base | $_____ | | |
| Commission | __% | $_____ Avg Sale × Commission = B | ___ Sales Needed |
| Average Sale Amount | $_____ | | |

Try funnel math for yourself!

CHAPTER 15

# IDEAL DAY

"I don't have time."

This might as well be the battle cry for underperforming salespeople. It's also one of the common myths I hear that consistently drives me crazy.

You probably know someone who loves to share how "busy" they are, and how they never seem to have enough time. Don't pity them. I once had a salesperson work for me that couldn't find the time to prospect, follow-up, or close business because they didn't have enough "time." They didn't last long.

First things first, you don't *make* more time. We all have twenty-four hours in the day, so let's take a look at how you could be spending it, but hopefully, are *not*.

- 8:15 a.m.—Arrive at the office, get coffee, get water, use the bathroom, eat breakfast at your desk, catch up with coworkers.

- 9:00 a.m.—Check personal email, then work email, check all social media, look at fantasy football standings and sports news. As soon as this cycle is done, repeat. Email to social media to sports news, and back to email again.

- 10:00 a.m.—Haphazardly start to work out of and respond to email, maybe even make a call or two, throw in a bathroom break, and another coffee.

- 11:30 a.m.—Better get ready to go to lunch. Check personal email, social media, sports news again (bathroom break, another coffee).

- 1:00 p.m.—Back to work, better repeat the cycle of email, chat with coworkers about lunch, personal emails, and finally get ready to work by logging into your systems.

- 2:00 p.m.—Ready to work, start with emails to follow-up on, make a few phone calls in between.

- 4:30 p.m.—Better start packing up, because you wouldn't want to stay any later than 5:01 p.m.

Keep in mind, this is a day without any meetings—internal or external!

If you say you don't have time, I don't give a shit. Make time. Work harder.

If I managed you, you'd be out the door.

If I were your coworker, I'd crush you.

I know the tricks of acting like you're busy. I get it—we all have days. But be honest with yourself and decide if you care. Do you? Cool, then keep reading.

Now you may think that this is an exaggeration, but I've worked with companies where this is the norm. If you're a business owner or sales leader in an organization and that outline of a day doesn't piss you off, you should be checked for a pulse. However, all across the United States, businesses are being drained by an underperforming sales force, whose day looks just like the one above.

The same people who are doing this are often the same ones who blame sales management, can't wait for the weekend, blame the company commission package, and complain they can never get ahead. These salespeople are everywhere.

The most common response to why salespeople don't do "more" is the lack of time. They don't have time to prepare, or follow-up appropriately, or close more deals. Let's be honest with each other.

**You have the time—everything else is an excuse.**

Let's develop an ideal daily schedule that will allow you to hit your Funnel Math numbers. Before we can do that, let's look at a typical 45-hour workweek:

**WEEKLY SCHEDULE**

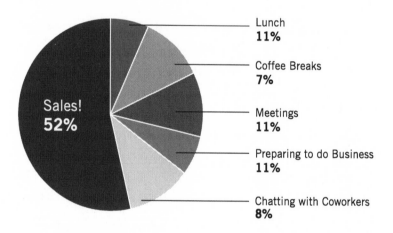

Lunch
**11%**

Coffee Breaks
**7%**

Sales!
**52%**

Meetings
**11%**

Preparing to do Business
**11%**

Chatting with Coworkers
**8%**

Out of a 45-hour week, you spend almost half (48 percent) in non-value-producing activities. Honestly, it probably is *more* than 48 percent in most offices. Some of this is unavoidable, but the above are extremely conservative estimates. The numbers could change on the person, but overall I believe that almost half of a salesperson's week is spent *not* selling.

Instead, let's build out your Ideal Day. Yes, by the hour because remember, discipline will set you free. People flounder without purpose and a plan. They dillydally because they don't have momentum. Remember college physics and Newton's First Law of Motion—an object at rest stays at rest and an object in motion stays in motion.

Here's an Ideal Day I recommend. Bonus: if you're really into it, block off your calendar daily with your Ideal Day schedule and treat it as an appointment with the CEO— don't miss it, focus and show up prepared.

- 8:00 a.m.—Get your coffee and connect with your coworkers so that you don't get distracted.

- 8:10 a.m.—Review tasks and your plan to tackle your day. Warning: you'll be tempted to jump into your inbox but be strong! Get your systems set so that you can start your high-producing activities.

- 8:30 a.m.—The Almighty Power Hour (See Chapter 16! This is a game changer!). This is your key time to focus on filling your pipeline and prospecting.

- 9:30 a.m.—Welcome to your inbox for the day. This is a great time to catch-up on returned calls and emails. Set yourself a timer and don't spend more than 60 minutes getting caught up in email. Remember, don't work out of your inbox. If you're finished early, make calls or start existing client follow-up. Don't sit idle.

- 10:30 a.m.—This is one of the core times that I recommend salespeople reserve for current client follow-up, demos for new leads, in-person appointments, etc. If you need to meet someone out of the office, this is a great time to do so because you already got your Almighty Power Hour in, and you'll be in a pumped-up state. Use this time to focus on making connections with your existing client base.

- 12:00 p.m.—Lunch, workout, run errands, get out of the office, read, or keep working!! At a minimum, get up and do something for a few minutes that's away from your desk to reboot your mind.

- 1:00 p.m.—Same as your 10:30 a.m. time block.

- 2:00 p.m.—Check your email for the afternoon, and then get ready to hit it again.

- 2:30 p.m.—Use these 30 minutes to develop your skills and expand your knowledge. There are activities throughout this book, like the Triangle

Drill (Chapter 19) and objection handling that can be incorporated into your week during this time. Getting better doesn't happen on its own—you have to practice to improve.

- 3:00 p.m.—Set yourself up for success tomorrow during this two-hour block. This is the time for prospect research. Get the names, numbers, and emails of people you plan on contacting. Spend time digging. Write new emails for your cadence. Outline your top five priorities for tomorrow and make sure you're ready to be open for business. With 15 minutes left in the workday, I like taking a few minutes to write everything down on my to-do list. It helps me brain dump any of my good ideas and tasks I need to do, so I can focus on being present with my family that evening.

- 5:00 p.m.—Go home or to happy hour.

I've implemented the Ideal Day concept across many teams, and the most challenging part of cutting over to this new way of operating and thinking is to separate oneself from email. I can already hear the people in your office say, "But, that's how we get sales, appointments—I have to respond." They're right, they do have to respond, but they don't have to react immediately. If you don't believe me, try for one day or afternoon and behold the freedom you'll take back from your inbox.

Have the discipline to follow your Ideal Day schedule, and the results will follow. You'll leave the office feeling accomplished versus wondering what you did all day.

## What do you want your day to look like?

| | |
|---|---|
| 7:00 AM | 1:00 PM |
| 8:00 AM | 2:00 PM |
| 9:00 AM | 3:00 PM |
| 10:00 AM | 4:00 PM |
| 11:00 AM | 5:00 PM |
| 12:00 PM | 6:00 PM |

CHAPTER 16

# THE ALMIGHTY POWER HOUR

If you're a business owner, sales leader or a quota-producing salesperson and you want to increase your results dramatically, one of the best things you can do is implement an Almighty Power Hour (as part of your Ideal Day) as quickly as possible. No, this is not the drinking game you may have played in college. It's a game changer for anyone who wants to work hard and smart!

**Either you control your day or the day controls you.**

Napoleon Hill coined this concept about controlling your mind, but it applies to your day as well. We all have the same twenty-four hours and no one is "too busy." It's just a matter of what you make a priority. The Almighty Power Hour forces salespeople and leadership to focus for sixty minutes a day on their most important tasks. I recommend no emails, no follow-up calls, no chit chat, no bathroom breaks, no instant messaging—only diving into your top priorities that will move the business forward.

Usually, when sales teams are introduced to this concept, they are less than thrilled. Typical objections include:

"What if I miss an important email?"

"What if I miss a deal?"

"What if...?"

"What if...?"

Before they have a chance to object, make sure you introduce the Almighty Power Hour like this:

1. Have everyone review their Dreamboard, Funnel Math and their Ideal Day.

2. Ask the question, "Do you feel that you'll be able to meet the required daily activities to reach your annual salary goal?" All good salespeople are motivated by money, so this should get them

thinking. Typically, this is a gut check. It dawns on them that what they want is a long way from what they're currently doing.

3. Then propose sixty minutes a day when everyone focuses on their top priorities— no distractions. It takes commitment from everyone, so they all hold each other accountable and so they all know to leave each other alone.

I've had the most battle-hardened, staunch email-reactive salespeople *hate* this idea when I first implemented it, but after only three days they love it. They love the freedom and structure it provides, and they love the results. Kicking off any new initiative like this can rock the boat, but it's worth it.

If you're an overachiever, start with sixty minutes and try to increase it by ten minutes every week. I've found that a morning and afternoon Almighty Power Hour yields the most productivity.

We live in a pretty distracting world, so for you to overcome these distractions, here are some tactics to stick to your Ideal Day and make the most of your Almighty Power Hour.

1. Turn off all phone notifications, especially social.

2. Turn off all desktop notifications on your computer (calendar, email, text, chat, social, etc.).

3. If you're in a private office, shut your door. If you're not, put a sign on the back of your chair that says "Do Not Disturb—Power Hour in Session."

4. When it comes time for your Almighty Power Hour, put your phone in a location you can't see it or put it upside down. Don't worry. It will still be there when you're done.

5. If you're in charge, have everyone in your company start using an Almighty Power Hour. Block off one hour per day, where no meetings can be scheduled and everyone focuses on their most important activity.

6. Time block the rest of your day so you have specific times for when you check email, have internal meetings, lunch, etc.

7. Have a start of day routine and an end of day routine.

8. Set a timer for yourself for how long you'll work on specific tasks.

Incorporating just a few of these tactics into your workday will increase productivity and renew mental clarity. Get off the hamster wheel of distraction, raise your standards, and own your day.

## CHAPTER 17

# KNOW THY BUYER

Another part of mise en place is to understand your buyer. In other words, doing prep work on who you are selling to. What do they care about? What is their background? Why would they want to buy from you? Before you talk to anyone, make sure your focus is on your best customers and prospects and how you can best help them.

I always say that salespeople operate the worst when the sky's the limit and opportunities are wide open. Salespeople need a narrow lane; otherwise they make the mistake of trying to be all things to all buyers. They try to call everyone because they think their product is phenomenal and can help everyone under the sun. Hooray for enthusiasm, but boo-hoo for spreading it too thin. It's a surefire way to go nowhere. Remember instead that there are riches in niches.

You could have the world's greatest product, but it doesn't mean anything if the person you're calling or meeting with is a poor fit for your product. It doesn't matter how much money it could save them, make them, or how much more efficient they could be by implementing your solution. None of that matters if it doesn't matter to them.

Many salespeople, business owners, and sales managers get a little defensive when I ask them to narrow their focus. Hello, scarcity mindset. The FOMO (fear of missing out, for you non-millennials) is real and they want to cast a "wide net" to make sure that they target all potential buyers.

Casting too wide of a net limits the efficacy of your sales, and ends up making it difficult for your sales team to truly target your best customers. If you have current inbound leads that aren't jiving with your ideal customer, work them through your funnel until either they purchase or are disqualified, but don't make it a habit.

Imagine if your boss upped your goal by $1M next year. Cool, you're up for the challenge. But where do you find prospects? Let's say you sell medical software. You could sell to every clinic, hospital, chiropractor, or dentist in North America. Or, you could get focused and target West Coast, outpatient clinics with 20-100 providers. That focus makes it way more doable, and *bam!* In no time, you have three hundred names you can call.

Again, it is *so* important to know thy buyer. I command you. Let's call it "Know Thy Buyer" or KTB from here on out. When you KTB you know the company or individual that will benefit from your service the most, pay you the highest rate, and will be excited to purchase your solution. Once you KTB with clarity, you know with whom you want to do business.

The more focused KTB, the more relevant and compelling sales messages you can tell. Today's buyer wants content and messaging created just for them. Mass messaging won't be as effective.

It's critical to know your audience, their concerns, what's happening in their marketplace, and what's happening with their competitors. This critical prep work demonstrates to your prospect that you're competent, professional, and that you actually give a damn about the conversation you're having. Yay for you!

If you've never experienced it before, I can tell you it's as frustrating as being stuck in rush hour traffic to sit with a sales rep who has no idea what your business does or even understands your market. It's a complete waste of time. Don't skip the prep—it's disrespectful. And momma didn't raise you to disrespect people. Note: In Chapter 26, we'll cover People Types, another helpful aspect of KTB.

**Know Thy Buyer**

Try this exercise to Know Thy Buyer. Start by answering these questions about your ideal customer avatar to help you stay focused. Remember this is just an avatar of the individual(s) and company you're going to target. This is not a real company and person you're asking these questions. However, be as descriptive as you absolutely can. It will help you better communicate with your "real" prospect and help you hone your sales messaging.

- What is their role or position?
- What are their goals?
- What are their values?
- Where do they get information from (Blogs, Websites, Conferences They Attend)?
- What are their possible objections to your solution or product?
- What is their company size?
- What market are they in?
- Who are their top competitors?
- What systems do they currently have in place?
- Who makes the buying decision?
- How many locations do they have?
- What problems are they trying to solve?
- What's happening in their industry?

The goal is to give you a laser-like focus on who's a good fit for you to spend your time targeting, contacting, and selling to, and who's not. The more focused your KTB is, the more focused your sales efforts can be.

It may seem a little crazy to think about and answer these questions for someone that doesn't exist, but bear with me on this exercise. I've had clients that name, add a picture of their KTB and the individual prospect. It's funny at first, but the results they get are not a laughing matter, they're crushing it. There's nothing like referring to a fictitious person in a meeting and being able to call them by name. Pretend you own an educational software company. Your KTB works in the school system in administration. Let's call him Steve the Superintendent, or her, Patty the Principal. Patty's goals are the safety of her students, keeping her budget in line, and providing world-class education and growth opportunities. Patty gets her information from trade publications and educator specific websites. Her "company size" is 350 teachers, administrative staff, and support. Her top competitors aren't your traditional sources for this example, but they could easily be online education, or students and parents transferring to other districts.

Do some deep work here and really think about your KTB. Be as descriptive as you absolutely can. There's no need to hold back or lay-up. Use as many descriptors and tidbits of info from your current favorite clients to inform your answers.

As you can see, the picture of our KTB comes into focus with more questions answered. The point of this exercise is to put yourself in the shoes of your buyer. Individuals and companies that excel at sales have a keen understanding of the pains, problems, and obstacles their buyer is facing every single day. They can articulate the problem that these companies and people are having to such a degree that the level of trust and credibility is instantly increased. This prep work is vital in understanding who you're really targeting and selling to and is the path to separating yourself from your competition.

CHAPTER 18

# SINK OR SWIM TEST

There's a great story about the legendary Coach John Wooden. For those that don't know the name...shame on you. Coach Wooden is widely recognized as the greatest and most successful coach of any sport in the history of human time as we know it. He's an impressive man professionally and personally, to say the least.

He coached the famed UCLA men's basketball team to an unprecedented ten National Championships, with seven of those championships coming in a row. And while he passed away in 2010 at the age of ninety-nine, his records and impact are still unbroken, and his leadership lessons are felt to this day. There's a classic Coach Wooden story retold by countless players that demonstrates the importance of mastering the basics.

The story goes like this. Every year, at the very first practice of the year, Coach Wooden would take all incoming freshmen and new players into the locker room for their first lesson. This is what they'd been waiting for. Their first real opportunity to learn from the "Wizard of Westwood." I can picture the locker room buzzing with excitement, anticipation, and nervous energy. The players were about to learn that their first lesson from the legendary coach was how to tie your shoes...not what they expected. Many of these players were All-Americans and some of the most sought-after athletes in the entire country, and Coach Wooden is teaching them something they learned in kindergarten!?

No joke. Coach Wooden spent the very first practice every season instructing his players how to properly put on socks, shoes, and properly lace up their Chuck Taylors. His theory was that if your shoes were not properly laced and your socks not properly protecting your feet, you were prone to blisters. Blisters meant that your performance would suffer, or worse, you wouldn't be able to play at all. You'd be useless to the team and the mission.

Even after winning his first, second, third, and up to his tenth National Championship in twelve years he still started every practice of every new season teaching his young players how to properly put on their socks, and lace up their shoes.

And if Coach Wooden can do it in basketball, you better believe you can do it in sales. Instead of cotton socks and laces, you can master your sales fundamentals.

How are you stressing the basics of your sales process and messaging? When was the last time you made sure that you or your entire team knew the core elements of your sales process, messaging, and value?

Drill and repetition lead to mastery. Even if you've been at the same company, selling the same product for years, you still need to cover the basics. Take a lesson from Coach Wooden and start sharpening your approach immediately with this test.

### Swim Test

I call it the Seven Question Sink or Swim Test. It allows everyone to stay sharp on the fundamentals, the basics...the "socks and shoes" of your company.

Everyone on your sales team (new, veteran reps, and yourself) should be able to answer the seven questions below with precision, crispness, and conviction. There should be consistency among the answers and a level of ownership and familiarity.

For new salespeople keep in mind that you're not asking them final Jeopardy questions. New salespeople should know this information after spending forty hours in your company. And if they don't, you haven't done an excellent job training them. A good salesperson who's proactive with adequate training should be able to answer these with the ease of knowing the lyrics to Journey's *Don't Stop Believin'* by the end of their first week.

### The Seven Question Sink or Swim Test

1. Briefly tell me about the main solution(s) we provide.
2. Give me three examples of our competition.
3. Name three of the most common objections we hear.
4. Tell me three things that make us unique, aka the most awesome company out there.
5. If we met at a bar or a backyard cookout, how would you describe our company?
6. What types of leads are not a good fit for solution or product?
7. Give me three qualifying questions you can ask to confirm that a lead is a good fit.

Here's what I'm looking for when I ask these questions to new reps. Answers to these questions don't have to be as polished as your top biller, but they do need to grasp the fundamental basics and do so confidently and with ease. Have they improved their knowledge since the interview process—i.e., do they know more than what's on your website? Can they rise to the occasion and perform under pressure? I also want to see a level of ownership that shows me they're critically thinking of the answers and how they tie into the overall business strategy. Did they spit back the company line, or do they demonstrate a deeper level of knowledge?

Mastering these basic, but critical questions for both new and experienced salespeople is all about demonstrating a firm understanding of the basics. If your new and experienced salespeople aren't crushing these questions, you need to rethink your sales training process and practice because it's not working.

This practice is like the other Standards discussed in this book. It may seem trivial and small, but buy-in and mastery have a much more significant cultural impact on the sales team and process.

## CHAPTER 19

# THE TRIANGLE DRILL

Think about the last appointment or pitch you had. How long did you spend researching the client? How much time did you spend thinking about your opening questions and secondary questions? How many times did you role practice with a coworker to try and simulate what kind of questions and responses the prospect may have for you?

Most people miss out on this crucial step of prep work. Practicing can be tough, especially when you have quotas to crush, and commission checks to cash. However, don't neglect this important action.

In my experience, the best salespeople are rehearsed, but *not* robotic. Think of any sports team, whether it's a professional golfer like Jordan Spieth (who I've seen in play at the Masters, us Open and Ryder Cup) or the beloved Green Bay Packers.

When they step out on the field, they've practiced the plays they're about to execute hundreds of times over the weeks and months previous.

To be the best, you have to practice. Practice opening lines, questions to keep the conversation rolling, questions to learn personal insight, questions that will reveal their buying motives, if they're the right person to be talking with, or if they can even make buying decisions.

And even though it sounds weird, the top salespeople practice more than just their questions. I've been with top performers who practice their entrance into a room, handshake, and smile. They don't leave anything to chance, because they know that someone's perception of their preparedness matters.

I've coached too many reps who think they'll show up, ask a few crappy questions, marginally listen, demo their product and expect the seven-figure sales to happen.

This is not how buyers work! Would you buy from you? Would you spend your hard-earned coin on your own sales presentation? Most reps, if they're honest with themselves, would say no.

The best salespeople have thought about what top objections they're going to have and how to overcome those objections. They don't wing it. They use the best response every single time. They don't deviate, and they close more business because of it. The best salespeople practice these rebuttals consistently until they have them memorized and can deliver the response with confidence and enthusiasm.

They get this confidence from practice. Not practicing on the prospect or client, but through deliberate practice with coworkers, spouses, and friends.

A simple exercise used to practice is something I call the Triangle Drill.

### The Triangle Drill

Have three people partner up. One becomes the client, one becomes the salesperson, and the last person is the observer. Practice your refined responses to standard objections and rotate until each person has had a turn.

You'll be amazed at the progress each person makes, primarily the observer. Every time I've recommended this drill to a new team I'm working with, I always get pushback and resistance. Usually, it sounds like this:

- "But, our sales process is too unique."
- "But, we have too many objections to count."
- "But, I need to have my research or notes or favorite beverage in front of me."
- "But it's cold outside, it's too hot outside, it's raining, it's sunny."
- "Do we *have* to do this?"

I have better luck convincing my young daughters to go to bed. If you're the sales leader, don't tolerate these excuses and don't back down. If you're a sales producer and are asked to do this, get on board. You will see results.

When I get pushback on this Drill, I always bring it back to the individual's goals. If they want to make six figures or earn an extra $25,000, I always remind them that what they've always done won't get them there. I ask them if their goal is still important, and then I ask if they've ever lost a sale due to mishandling an objection. I then ask if they've ever lost a sale—period.

This usually brings someone back to the importance of why we're doing this.

So the Triangle Drill it is.

Practice until your questions, responses, and movement through the conversation is second nature. Once you have mastered this skill, you'll have confidence during the meeting because you know what to expect. You can rely on your training, sit back, and be present in your conversation, asking great questions, and building stellar rapport.

## CHAPTER 20

# YOUR BEST SOCIAL SELF

Think back to the last time you were getting pitched by someone. Did you Google their name and company? Did you look them up on social media? Of course, you did.

So, if you're doing this to others, don't you think the leads you're calling on are doing this to you? Of course, they are.

Tell me. What perception could others get from checking out your Instagram page? Do you stand out on LinkedIn or do you blend into the sea of business suits, stiff titles, and zero personality? When they Google you, what do they find?

Wake up! Most prospects don't even respond until they've done their research on you, your company, and your product. Buyers are more knowledgeable and more connected than ever.

First, create a social personality. The best version of you online. Get yourself some social credibility, dude or dudette. Delete those pictures of you getting drunk at a tailgate or those unfortunate Vegas bachelor party pics. Remember, all of this is found online. But you knew that already.

Once you've cleaned up the house party, be intentional about how you use social. Is it a resume or a sales tool? Are you looking for a new job or making magic happen in the position you already have?

Remember what Jeffrey Gitomer said, "All things being equal, people want to do business with their friends. And all things being *not* so equal, people *still* want to do business with their friends."

My greatest tip and challenge to you is this...craft a "Signature Move."

Your "Signature Move" will build rapport with people even if you're not talking to them. It will open up the conversation and get you connected faster with other like-minded individuals. It will help you stick out from the masses and make you memorable. People like people, not online profiles and postings. Be a real person!

So here's how you craft it.

**Signature Move**
Ponder the answers to these questions:

- Why'd you get into the industry you're in?
- Who are you doing it for?
- What's something a good friend would say that you're really into?
- Who are your favorite sports teams?
- What is your favorite snack? Candy? Drink?
- What's your superpower?
- What are you usually guilty of bringing to a party?

Review your answers and pick one thing (*one* thing) that you want to talk about all the time, and be known for it online. You'll get sick of talking about it, but to others it's a mental trigger that you're awesome. This "Signature Move" will be sprinkled into your social profiles, emails, and more. It should remind people of you instantly when they come across it, and people might even start to associate it with you even when they are *not* at work. You might be getting emails from random people saying, "I saw this and it made me think of you." Bingo. Your Signature Move is working! Warning: Keep it professional and know your audience.

If you're confused, here are some examples I've come across. I'm sure this will get your mind going, but do *not* be a copycat. You be you. You are unique and memorable and kick ass. So make your Signature Move about *you*.

- You always wear hipster yellow glasses.
- You love coffee...pour over, French press, AeroPress...and make an ethically sourced cup every morning.
- You live by the water and love to surf, kayak, stand up paddleboard, or sail.
- You are obsessed with the Green Bay Packers.
- You are an advocate for juvenile diabetes.
- You always wear bow ties.
- You are a guacamole aficionado.
- You volunteer with local nonprofits.

You might not think this thing about yourself is interesting. You might think it makes you regular. But, pick something and make it your Signature Move.

The second step to establishing your social cred is to find your vehicle. Where do you want to hang out online? It's easy to get overwhelmed with all of the options—Facebook, Instagram, Twitter, Snapchat, LinkedIn, blog posts, podcasts, YouTube, and the list will be forever changing. Then, you have to decide if you like to write, record videos, speak into a microphone, or create visuals. Yeah...it's a lot.

But, you don't have to dominate or even be in all of these channels to start moving the needle. Pick one channel where your audience congregates. If you're selling enterprise-level software to Fortune 500 companies, LinkedIn is your best bet. If you're selling a consumer product to mothers, Facebook or Instagram is going to be your top choice. If you want to educate people, maybe YouTube or a podcast could be fun.

You don't have to become a production machine. Instead, create a few pieces of content relevant to what you're selling, and what your buyer finds interesting. Make sure your Signature Move comes up every few posts and be consistent. Stick to a schedule and make it a non-negotiable. Most people are just lurkers on social. They consume but are anonymous. It's easy to stand out if you just put yourself out there. Also, this is different than your corporate social strategy. This is only for your personal brand. Yes, *you*. I know how awkward and vulnerable it can be to put yourself out there online, but it's better than blending into the masses.

Don't overlook this aspect of prep work because people want to buy from people that they know, like, and trust. Building a positive online presence is one of the easiest ways for people to like you, even if they've never met you.

STANDARD 3:

SELLING

"It is not the critic who counts; not the man who points out how the strong man stumbles, or where the doer of deeds could have done them better. The credit belongs to the man who is actually in the arena, whose face is marred by dust and sweat and blood; who strives valiantly; who errs, who comes short again and again, because there is no effort without error and shortcoming; but who does actually strive to do the deeds; who knows great enthusiasms, the great devotions; who *spends himself in a worthy cause; who at the best knows in the end the triumph of high achievement, and who at the worst, if he fails, at least fails while daring greatly, so that his place shall never be with those cold and timid souls who neither know victory nor defeat."*

—Teddy Roosevelt, 1910

The man in the arena holds a special place in my heart. To me, it's a salesperson who continues to work hard no matter the weather, time of year, or distraction. The salesperson whose hard work builds and grows a company call by call, account by account.

Without sales, companies don't exist.

It's not for the faint of heart. Anyone who tells you different is lying. At its best, it can deliver a life of wealth and accomplishment. At its worst, it's demoralizing and defeating. But the lows make the highs that much sweeter.

The Standards in this section were developed in rebellion to the old way of selling that I see so many good-meaning salespeople fall victim to. The old way of selling wants to trick, cajole, and manipulate people into buying. If you've ever fallen prey to this "technique," you know how repelling this can be.

Every time I find myself in this situation, it feels like I need a shower. You too?

Or maybe you've experienced the old way of selling by means of a salesperson so enamored with their product (and commission) that they recite a bunch of product information without asking a single question or giving a damn about your opinion. They might have been talking to a brick wall because that's about how much collaboration they were looking for. It's nauseating.

Listen, this is the old way of selling, and it has to stop.

Standard 3: Selling is dedicated to the actual art of...yes, the *new* way of selling! You can have the best Prep Work, but if you can't sell and close when the lights are on and the cameras are rolling, your sales profession could be brief.

Think of it this way, Standard 2: Prep Work happened back in the kitchen, behind the scenes. Standard 3: Selling occurs in the dining room of a restaurant. Prep Work is your mise en place. Selling is the actual dinner, the meat and potatoes—being engaged in conversation, listening, and being a nice human who adds value and doesn't sell someone something they don't need.

## Selling Standards

- Use your Playbook
- Execute the Four-Part Sales Method
- Part 1: Build Rapport with Everyone You Talk To
- Part 2: Ask Questions and Listen
- Part 3: Speak to Answers
- Part 4: Win-Win
- Understand People Types

## CHAPTER 21

# USE YOUR PLAYBOOK

Let me warn you. This section contains actionable content that can have a major impact on your sales. But, there's only one way to tackle it—one section at a time. This chapter will challenge you to really think through what your sales system should be. I'll be laying out a step-by-step guide of how to have great sales conversations that will empower you and your sales team.

Ever feel like your sales go up and down without any control? It's as if sales only come if the stars align and their zodiac sign is right. At every organization and with countless sales teams the common theme I hear is that sales can be "inconsistent."

News flash. Inconsistent sales come from a poor pipeline. Poor pipelines come from a lack of *understanding* your pipeline and not having enough prospects. If you want a consistent conveyor belt of hot deals flowing in your direction, there's no magic, only work.

In this section you're going to get clarity on your pipeline, so you can accurately plot your prospects in the funnel. From there you can come up with action items at each level of the funnel, making your sales process consistent and scalable. We'll call this your Playbook, filled with qualification questions, discovery questions and more...all the way down to the email written or the call script to use. As a salesperson, there's nothing better than knowing what your next step is in the sales process. As a sales leader, having insight into what's working for your sales team's process vs. what's working "in theory" is a powerful tool.

Having this Playbook ready to follow instead of your current method of "praying and spraying" is gold. While every company's Playbook will look different, at its core it should cover the essential tasks done at the top, middle, and bottom of your funnel. We'll go through each section of your funnel so you have a clear understanding of what activities and actions you or your sales team will be taking at every turn. If you've always wondered what to do next, or are confused as to the next step in the sales journey, then look no further and follow a Playbook.

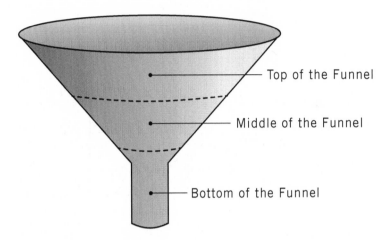

Here's the framework:

- Top of the Funnel
    - Goal = Create awareness, fill the funnel with leads and qualify potential buyers
    - Activities Look Like = Outbound, proactive communication

- Middle of the Funnel
    - Goal = Educate KTB, highlight the problems and paint your solution as the hero
    - Activities = Demo, appointments, presentations

- Bottom of the Funnel
  - Goal = Create urgency, get lead to take action
  - Activities = Hold KTB's hand across the finish line

## TOP OF THE FUNNEL

So first, let's talk about the top of the funnel. The goal here is creating awareness. How do you acquire leads? Is it up to you to fill the funnel, or is a marketing and/or sales minion doing it for you? Are the leads organic, from a list building service, social media, email marketing, LinkedIn, lead magnets, trade shows, or lead sharing? Are you hunting for new leads or farming existing leads? Are you diving deep or going wide? The answers to these are not either/or statements. They are *yes and* statements. Meaning, you need to go wide *and* deep. You need to hunt *and* farm. Do it all and fill the funnel with people who align with your KTB.

### FILL YOUR FUNNEL

One of the most critical elements of any business is buyers, right? So of course, any company I speak to would love to have more prospects or leads in their funnel. But, wanting more and doing something about it are two different things. Sadly, most businesses that I work with don't have a systematic approach to how they're going to get leads. Do they think the funnel magically fills up and leads come knocking on their door? No. In their dreams.

But then where do businesses find prospects, you might ask? Great question. Don't get bogged. There are hundreds of different opportunities. Start by concentrating on where your KTB is located.

B2B companies can be found on:

- LinkedIn
- Social Media
- Hoover's
- Dun & Bradstreet
- Chamber of Commerce
- Industry Groups and Societies
- Local Business Journal
- Networking Events
- Trade Shows
- Sharing leads with partners or colleagues (noncompetitors that share the same audience)

For B2C try to find where your buyers hang out via:

- Social media sites and the millions of groups that people identify themselves as a member of
- Meetup groups or clubs
- Consumer events
- Publications and magazines
- Websites dedicated to that niche

There are also dozens of organizations that build and sell lists based off of your unique market.

This small list of ideas will begin to help you find leads. But, it's not about the leads, it's about what you're going to do with them once you get the lead.

I'll say it again. It's not about the source. It's about the action post-acquisition.

You can have one thousand leads in your pipeline and bomb the follow-up, wasting them and missing out on opportunity. Or you can have fifty leads to nurture and serve, execute a great cadence and follow-up strategy, and earn an 80 percent close rate!

One of the common things holding most sales teams and salespeople back from making more prospecting calls and outreach is that they don't know what to say or how to handle a new lead. Enter a cadence.

## CADENCE

A cadence will be your best friend because it takes the guesswork out of how, when, and by what method to contact your prospect. The best cadences use a variety of methods to reach a prospect. For example, below is a successful cadence that I've implemented many times. This fifteen-day cadence shows a salesperson calling and emailing a lead nine times. (I'll give you the scripts in a few pages.) Of course, this is only if the prospect does not respond. If you have twenty leads, apply this cadence to every single lead individually.

It may sound daunting or too aggressive, but today's executive is getting absolutely inundated with emails, text messages, social media posts, and calls. Your job as a salesperson is to break through that noise, as if saying, *"You need to pay attention to me."*

Here's an example of a successful cadence:

| | |
|---|---|
| Day 1 | Call, Voicemail, Email |
| Day 2 | Call, Voicemail, Email |
| Day 3 | Call, Voicemail, Email |
| Day 4 | Call, Voicemail, Email |
| Day 5 | Call, Voicemail, Email |
| Day 7 | Call, Voicemail, Email |
| Day 9 | Call, Voicemail, Email |
| Day 13 | Kiss-Off 1 |
| Day 15 | Kiss-Off 2 |
| Monthly | Call, Voicemail, Email |

I've implemented this cadence in vastly different industries including B2B and B2C businesses. The results are always the same. We see a massive increase in connections, meetings generated, pipeline growth, and revenue created. Here's why. The amount of activity prescribed in this cadence along with the frequency of touches breaks through to the prospect.

Another key element of this cadence is something I'll refer to as a pattern. A pattern is the "how" of a cadence. Most underperforming salespeople that I work with typically only use one form of communication when they're trying to get in touch with a prospect. Usually it's an email or phone call. They'll leave a voicemail or send an email, then wait for a response. This will *not* break through the noise.

I recommend a pattern approach when you're going to reach out to a prospect. So when it's time on the Cadence to contact the lead, you should call, leave a voicemail, and email all within two minutes. The importance of this process cannot be overstated. Do not take the easy road out and only leave a voicemail or just send an email. The power in the cadence and utilizing a pattern is in the amount of *and* method of communication. One email or voicemail is too easy to delete. However, if you leave a call, leave a voicemail, and email all within two minutes, this will stand out.

Remember when we talked about The Almighty Power Hour? Use this time to work prospects through this cadence using patterns. First, no matter what else happens in your day, you'll have moved some prospects through your pipeline, and success in sales occurs over time with repeated daily actions. Second, if you have your Almighty Power Hour first thing in the day, which I recommend, you'll have notched a win, and that will bring momentum to your day. The last thing any salesperson usually wants to do is make cold contact, so do that right away to get it off your mind.

I always joke with my team, "Reach out until your prospect buys, dies or calls the cops." This isn't sleazy or overly aggressive. It's what has to be done to break through the noise. Subtle hints do not work in sales. Your high school girlfriend might have received a letter on loose-leaf paper, and that sealed the deal. But today's buyer needs flowers, a lovey-dovey note, a phone call, and balloons in first-period English class. Remember, this is sales. You want to win.

So you love the idea of a cadence, now let's talk about what you're going to say in the cadence.

## CADENCE SCRIPTS

It's been my experience that a lot of salespeople have some anxiety when it comes to reaching out to cold or lukewarm prospects. Often, this stems from a lack of confidence in what to say if the prospect picks up the phone. This leads to anxiety, procrastination, and eventually to avoiding the call. That's not good. So, do yourself a favor and have a plan of what to say and keep it simple.

Here's a baseline, but customize as you test and refine to your style and company culture.

### Cold Call

**Prospect Answers:** *Hi, is [Prospect's Name] there?*

**Intro:** *Hi, [Prospect Name], this is [Your Name] at [Your Company], how are you doing?*

**Transition:** *In a nutshell, we help [department] teams solve [major problem]. Do you have three minutes?*

**Value + Story:** *We help [KTB] with [problem] by [solution]. You might find this interesting, we recently [example of how you helped another customer].*

*Are you in a similar situation? How are you handling [problem]? Is this [problem] concerning you?*

**Gain Commitment:** *It sounds like there's value in having a larger conversation about this. Are you available for a longer discussion this week or next week?*

*Does earlier or later in the week typically work better for you? Morning or Afternoon? And what's the best email to send a calendar invite to?*

**Gratitude:** *Thanks for your time today! I look forward to our chat next week.*

Keep this conversation clear and to the point. If the conversation is going really well, you can elaborate on some of your success stories and go deeper with your conversation. Remember your ideal outcome in this conversation is a second appointment or scheduling a demo. Make sure you have a clear call to action (CTA) in your conversation. I also recommend confirming this conversation with a calendar invite and sending a quick thank you email.

If the lead doesn't pick up, I recommend leaving a voicemail for every single call. And here's why—you want to reinforce and stand out from the masses, not blend in. Keep the voicemail simple and to the point. With visual voicemail, barely anyone will listen to your long-winded voicemail. And no one is buying from your pseudo two-minute pitch on their voicemail. Get in, get out! Here's what I say.

### Voicemail Script

*This is [name]. Please give me a call back at [number].*

I like to get straight to the point when it comes to voicemails. I do this because if you've followed the cadence the prospect should have received your calls and emails. Reinforce the point that you're trying to reach them and move on.

### Email Scripts

In the pattern, I recommend pairing a phone call with an email. It allows you to get your name in front of the prospect in more than one way. Here are seven examples to send within ninety seconds of getting someone's voicemail.

Do not send the same email every day of the cadence! Customize each one. I like to add case studies, links to relevant articles, and quick emails that remind them of your previous email. Remember, it doesn't have to be overly complicated. Keep it simple. Be human. Add in some humor or fun, depending on your industry or personality.

Some additional intriguing subject lines I've seen are:

- [Name] suggested I reach out
- I'll Cut to The Chase
- "Contacting you at [Referral]'s suggestion"
- "If you're experiencing [common pain point], you're not alone"
- [Name], Going to [Event]?

### Example 1

*Subject:* [Prospect Name], I just missed you

Hey [First Name],

When can we talk? I just tried calling, but I'm guessing you're busy!

To boil it down, we help [department, or position] solve [major problem or achieve this major goal].

If this is a [problem or goal] you're looking to [solve or achieve], please call me back at [number] or reply here and let me know if there's a better time for you?

Let's talk soon.

[Signature]

## Example 2

*Subject:* [First Name], Need to Accomplish X?

Hey [First Name],

Is increasing X, decreasing Y] important to you?

[Company] offers [tools or services] for [business] just like yours that include the following:

[Main Feature #1 and how it helps]

[Main Feature #2 and how it helps]

[Main Feature #3 and how it helps]

Interested?

[Signature]

## Example 3

*Subject:* [Prospect Name], imagine life with [major benefit]

I know you're busy so I'll get straight to the point.

We have a client who was struggling with [problem]. Sound familiar? With our solution they're now experiencing [major benefit].

Imagine what your [c-level/management/board] would think if your business [major solution]?

Curious how they did it?

I'll call you tomorrow to explain...I promise the call will only take 5 minutes!

[Signature]

## *Example 4*

*Subject:* [First Name], let's chat

Hey [Name],

I know things can get lost in the clutter. Let's chat soon.

All the best,

[Signature]

## *Example 5*

*Subject:* [First name]...

Should I keep reaching out about [solution]?

## *Example 6*

*Subject:* Is there someone else I should talk to?

[Name],

I'm following up on my last email. I didn't hear back from you, everything ok? If it makes sense to talk, let me know when you're free.

If not, who is the appropriate person for me to talk to?

Thanks for your help,

[Signature]

*Example 7*

*Subject:* [First name], is this still a priority?

Hello [Name],

I haven't heard from you in a while. Should I just assume that [product/service] isn't a priority right now?

If so, I'll check back in six months or so to see if this has moved up in priority.

Thanks,

[Signature]

You may have also noticed the final two emails of the cadence are called "kiss-off" emails. A kiss-off email is where you're basically giving the prospect notice. You're creating some urgency and scarcity in an attempt to get them to call you or email you back. Here's an example of what a kiss-off email can look like:

[Prospect Name],

I know you've gotten at least five of my attempts to start a conversation. I'm guessing that you fall into one of the categories below:

1. Kidnapped by pirates and being held for ransom. Yikes!

2. Interested, but just too busy to respond.

3. Not interested at this time...check back in a few months.

Can you let me know which category you fall into right now by simply replying with a 1, 2, or 3?

P.S. You can use the link in my signature and schedule a time for us to connect.

You'd be amazed at how successful this email is at getting a response.

Remember, the whole goal of the top of the funnel is two things—(1) connect with qualified prospects and (2) get them to either:

- Agree to and schedule an in-person demo, phone call, or presentation
- Decline because they're not a fit for your services or product (but make sure it's a *real* reason)

Now that you've gained a commitment from prospects for a demo or meeting, let's introduce the middle part of the funnel.

## MIDDLE OF FUNNEL

The middle of the funnel may look different for different businesses, but at its core this is the part of the funnel where the prospect has awareness about you and your company, and the next logical step in the funnel is to understand their needs on a deeper level and introduce your product or service. This can happen either through a scheduled call, in-person appointment, or an online demo where you walk the lead through your product or solution and how it relates to their needs, desires, and wants.

I'll talk mainly about scheduling and conducting an online demo, but this applies just as much to an exploratory conversation or in-person meeting.

## HOW DO I PREPARE?

First, before you're going to demo or meet with a person, I recommend knowing who you're dealing with. Of course you have a general idea of the company and the people you're meeting with, but this is the stage to take a deeper dive into the company. Make sure you have baseline information that can assist you in asking better questions and coming fully prepared. Early in my career, I made the mistake of "winging it" and not doing any prep work for appointments. My ego and paycheck took a beating. Don't rely on your wit, charm, and personality. Don't leave it to chance. Have some understanding of the people whose time you're taking!

You should have a good baseline from the work you did in Chapter 17: Know Thy Buyer. Take it one step further and spend a couple of minutes thinking about the company and the other person or people that you're going to be communicating with. What are the common problems you solve? How do you help employees of the company that you serve?

Here's a quick checklist that you should have complete before any meeting or demo:

- Company Name (sounds silly, but you'd be surprised)
- Person's Name (yes, you'd be surprised *again!*)
- Flagship Product
- Who are their customers?
- Who are their competitors?

Second, before the demo reach out at least twenty-four hours in advance and re-introduce yourself, as well as share any helpful materials beforehand. This strategy helps re-establish any connection that you previously had, and shows that you're prepared.

Third, you need to practice your demo. I would much rather have my sales team practice on each other than I would have them practice on a client or prospect that could pay money for your service or product. Build into your schedule opportunities for your team to practice demos and you'll be amazed at how much of an improvement you'll see. Maybe once a quarter? Rotate a sales rep each month?

You can even improve your demos by creating a library of A+ demos. This helps veteran and new reps alike learn the best practices without having to sit in on a live demo. Having a library of great demos or calls will also help onboard new hires and give them an expectation and goal.

## WHAT DO I SAY?

Do not just "show-up and throw-up" the entire time, and don't just rattle on about your product. Use the first several minutes in the conversation to evaluate and qualify the need. Make sure that your prospect is still a good fit, allowing you to tailor your demo to their specific needs.

After you Build Rapport (see Chapter 22), transition into the evaluation part of the conversation:

- "Last time we talked, [problem] was impacting your business, is that still the case?"
- "What do you hope to get out of our conversation today?"
- "Let's make sure that we're not wasting each other's time. Let me ask you a couple of questions to make sure we're still a potential fit."
- "What do you need to see today, to make this call a success?"
- "What are you most interested in learning about today?"

Then you should go into qualifying questions. Take the information you learned from any past conversations or research to influence your conversation. These next questions should really highlight the issue or the current state your prospect is in. Here are some I like to ask:

- What's causing the [problem] we discussed on the phone?
- Why are you interested in our solution or product?
- What do you know about our company or solution?
- What's been your experience trying to solve [major problem]?
- If in two years you could have [major problem] solved, what do you think would have to happen to solve it?
- Have you used anything like [solution] in the past? How'd it go?

I recommend asking these questions on every new demo. Add more questions that will help best qualify your prospects. Getting your prospects to answer each of the questions honestly is a perfect world scenario and won't always happen. So, keep in mind that they will never answer any question that you *don't* ask. So even if you think it's awkward, ask the questions.

## HOW DO I PRESENT?

Once you've qualified your prospects, you can move on to demoing your product. Here are my 12 Rules of Giving a Great Demo:

1. Always start with something that's going to grab their attention—customer stories or impressive statistics
2. Never "feature dump," no one cares

3. Focus on the main challenges that your customer is experiencing

4. Do not get into the technical weeds of your product unless that was the only purpose of the demo

5. Be enthusiastic

6. Don't use confusing jargon

7. Never interrupt a question from your prospect

8. Don't ever assume

9. Never lie, it's a thousand times better to say you don't know than to pretend you have an answer

10. Look for ways to involve your prospect during the conversation

11. Always close with a recap of your top three highlights or most important takeaways

12. Never leave a demo without a commitment and time for the next appointment

Don't overcomplicate it. Remember that throughout the demo you should be qualifying the prospect as much as they're qualifying your product or solution.

## HOW DO I FOLLOW-UP AFTER A DEMO?

One of the key elements of the demo is what happens *after* the actual demo, but so many people miss out on this critical step. Excellent demo follow-up is a great way to stand out from the crowd. And remember, how you follow-up is a clear indication of how you'll do business once a prospect becomes a client.

After gaining the commitment of next steps after your demo, always send an email that confirms what you covered, what the main takeaways were, and summarize what the next steps are with dates and times. This is also a great time to follow-up with any testimonials, case studies, or ROI calculators that you either discussed in your presentation or are most applicable. This establishes expectations and saves you time if what you plan on doing is not what your prospect desires.

When it comes to following up with pricing, I believe that pricing should be conveyed either over the phone, in person, or on Skype. Sure it raises your anxiety when it comes to talking about price, and it's uncomfortable for most people, but don't fall into the trap of just sending an email and hoping that they accept.

When we discuss price on the phone, for example, I'll send all other relevant information they wanted and then schedule a quick chat to discuss pricing. I find that when given the ability to talk someone through pricing or a quote, you can flush out any initial objections and overcome any confusion. This is also a great time to confidently remind them of the value or cost savings experienced with your solution.

## WHEN DO I CUT THE PROSPECT LOOSE?

It's happened to just about everyone in the sales profession. You deliver a great demo, the prospect seems like an ideal fit, and then they go dark. No message, call, or Dear John letter, they just all of a sudden vanish! It's normal, in the middle of funnel, for prospects to shop around and evaluate with both long and short timelines.

Don't take it personally. Look back at your interactions and see if you held to your KTB criteria. Were they actually a good prospect, or did you just think they were? People fall out and go dark for a variety of reasons that often don't have anything to do with you. A lot of salespeople that I talk to take this as a personal offense and jump to the conclusion that the prospect obviously hated their product and them. *Stop* being so whiny! Prospects often drop out for their own reasons, like they took on a new project, family life is crazy, or here's a shocker...they're busy! Stop thinking you're the center of their universe. The world doesn't revolve around you and your product. Quit taking the lack of response as personal, and keep calling and emailing until you get a response. They will respond, don't stop.

Meanwhile, make sure that you have a robust pipeline so that if your top two deals in the middle of your funnel do this to you, it won't ruin your month or quarter. Put these contacts in your monthly follow-up plan (covered in Chapter 27) and move on for now. Don't spend too much time worrying, find more KTBs and reload!

It's not the customers that say no to you that hurt your business. It's the ones that say maybe and take up your time and attention. Make sure that you safeguard against these "maybe" clients.

## BOTTOM OF FUNNEL

Well, you've got them this far, you might as well make them a customer.

If you've taken the time to really identify who can best use your service, you've reached out to them in a systematic approach and you had a compelling demo, you should be progressing deals through to the bottom of your pipeline with some frequency. Your buying cycle might be two weeks or two years, but regardless this is the general process of most sales funnels.

Let's be clear on the bottom of the funnel. You don't control when someone buys. That's their decision, not yours. And like I've said before, people buy for their own reasons. With all that being said, you can still help influence the situation in a positive way.

There are four key elements to the bottom of the funnel:

1. Close without desperation
2. Have a list of ideas and methods you can employ to move the needle and close deals
3. Know how to handle objections
4. Never be afraid to upsell or cross-sell

## CLOSE WITHOUT DESPERATION

The goal in the bottom of the funnel is to *win*. Close the deal. Hook the whale. But, here's the catch. If you don't have enough in your pipeline, you ooze desperation and neeeeeed the deal to close, which is probably one of the biggest sales turnoffs possible. Don't act like a middle school boy desperately trying to get girls to dance with you. It's unsightly, and we all feel bad for you. If you don't think your prospect doesn't pick up on this, you're dead wrong. They know, and they'll build up walls to fend you off. So, never be in the position where if your top two deals fall out, you're totally screwed without the proverbial paddle.

Closing with desperation looks a lot like calling multiple times to just "check-in" or sending emails that say, "just wanted to check the status." Don't waste your time, or your prospect's time. Add value instead of being desperate.

## MOVE THE NEEDLE

One method to save time, increase autonomy, and increase sales is to develop a list of tactics that are approved through management that can be used to influence a deal—we'll call this a "move the needle" list. Don't just leave it up to chance for deals to close. You need to get out there and make it happen.

Make sure the "move the needle" list ideas create urgency and scarcity—two powerful marketing motivator concepts. Some examples of these are:

- Create a deadline on each of your offers
- Limit enrollment periods
- Limit the spots, or products you can offer
- Illustrate impact on how much your solution or product will help

Here are some other ideas to "move the needle":

### *Email from the* CEO

Hello [Prospect],

I just got out of a conversation with [your name] your [your position title]. We're excited at the prospect of working with you and I just wanted to reach out. If you need anything, don't hesitate to reach me directly.

Thanks,

[CEO Signature]

### *Notecard and Pen*

Hey [First Name],

We're really looking forward to working with you and the next step is for you to sign off on our contract/agreement. I've included a fresh new pen in case you lost yours! :)

[Signature]

*Scarcity Email*

Hey [Prospect Name],

Last time we talked, you expressed an interest in [product or service]. I wanted to let you know that we only have [amount] left or [are currently booking work out until]. If you're still interested, you'll need to act fast. I can only hold your spot a few days longer.

Let me know what we can do to make this deal a no-brainer for you.

[Signature]

## KNOW HOW TO HANDLE OBJECTIONS

The bottom part of the funnel has many different pitfalls and objections that could lead to the loss of sales. However, this is where the stakes are at their highest. You've already dedicated a lot of time, effort, and energy into getting them this far, so don't be tripped up by something you could have practiced. When it comes to handling objections of why people don't buy from you, that can be a little more complicated as you may need to overcome a multitude of objections.

Receiving objections in this stage of the funnel signals that you're moving through roadblocks or potential issues on your way to the sale. View these objections as mile markers on your way to getting the deal done. Regardless of how many objections you'll face, make sure that you have a best-practiced response for responding. Don't get caught flat-footed!

Think of this activity as understanding how to respond to objections. Don't forget about Chapter 19: Triangle Drill, which gives you a fun way to practice objection handling with your team.

## WHY PEOPLE DON'T BUY

**Objections and responses**

| Objection | Best Response |
|---|---|
| 1. We really like your competitor's solution. | Tell me, what do you like best about this solution? |
| 2. It's not the right time. | That's what a lot of my best current clients said before we showed them _____. |
| 3. The price is too high. | Too high compared to what? Is it a cash flow issue or a budget issue? Let's say money wasn't an object, would our product or service help you solve your problem? |
| 4. *Insert your own objections/responses.* | |
| 5. | |

## DON'T BE AFRAID TO UPSELL

One of the best times to cross-sell or upsell a product or service is when the prospect just bought and turned into a customer. Think about it. The time to hit them up for an even greater level of service or product is the time when they just felt the victory of buying! You know that feeling. The feeling of elation after making a great purchase that will positively impact your life. Years ago, I bought my first carbon fiber triathlon bike. When the company asked if I wanted to upgrade my order to their triathlete package, including a wetsuit, helmet, and accessories, I couldn't throw my credit card at them fast enough.

Before you even attempt to upsell, you've got to believe that the upsell is valuable. How many times have you been asked to purchase a warranty (unconvincingly and unenthusiastically) from the clerk checking you out at your local electronics store? My knee-jerk reaction is obviously going to be "no" because he or she gave me all the signals not to buy it!

Don't try to sell too many things. Focus on the most logical upsell product that you can offer. Then don't leave it to chance. Script out exactly when and how you're going to say those magical words and actually do it. Most salespeople don't want to mess up the deal or think that by offering them even more, they'll get upset and cancel the whole order. This never happens, and if you have a higher way you can help your prospect, and if they're a good fit for the product or service, it's your obligation to offer it to them.

The great part about this Playbook is that it gives your salespeople a process to follow so they know where and how they can best move prospects through the pipeline. Each company and industry will be different, and some may be much shorter than this process. Take the guidelines and fundamentals above and apply them to your business. Remember, if you don't have a system, you can't improve upon that system. Keep metrics of where different deals fall out over time and develop those parts of your funnel.

Don't make it more complicated than what it needs to be. This Playbook only works if you do. A lot of salespeople and business leaders want to trick themselves into thinking that if they build a good product, people will flock in masses. But history tells us that great products don't guarantee sales or success. You *need* sales or you're destined for the business graveyard.

I know that roughly 20 percent of readers will take the Playbook seriously and do the hard work it takes to implement the cadence. The other 80 percent will find excuses, like the people who get bicep implants instead of just doing some arm exercises. Side note: are bicep implants really a thing?! For the 20 percent that are going to take action on this book, and not look for shortcuts, I salute you.

For the 80 percent, I know that you want more. I know that every Sunday evening, as you flop down on your couch to watch football, *Game of Thrones*, or anything else you can find to take your mind off the nauseating feeling Monday morning has in store for you, that you dread heading back into work because you're not where you want to be. You panic before any sales meeting, thinking that this could be your last. You could change it all, if you wanted to bad enough.

I know this is a giant chapter and it leaves you with a lot to implement and start working on. But you now have the Playbook that's been responsible for generating millions in sales revenue for companies of all shapes and sizes. It can work for you as well, but it needs to be implemented and it definitely won't happen by itself. With that in mind, I recommend you take some time to review the previous chapter and the different recommendations I have in each part of the funnel before moving on.

Over the next five chapters I'm going to explain the four main components of an excellent sales interaction. This will offer a whole new aspect on selling that you may have always known was out there, but weren't able to put into words. We're going to go deep into my Four-Part Sales Method and People Types. In the Method, you're going to be given a road map to having better sales interactions with any type of person, including those "types of people" you've struggled to work with in the past. I'll give you the exact guide to having an awesome sales conversation turning prospects into buyers. Let's dive in.

## CHAPTER 22

# BUILD RAPPORT

If I gave you the option of purchasing a product or service from someone you had some connection with vs. someone who you know nothing about, which would you choose? Most people would choose the first option because it's human nature to want to do business with people that we like. When we know, like and trust people, it's easy to build rapport. But, have you ever been in a conversation where there is absolutely no rapport? Pretty awkward, right?

From a tactical standpoint, the opening parts of a phone conversation with a prospect are a great time to start the rapport building. You don't have to dwell on it, but I recommend not skipping it. If you're meeting in person, you can use the walk from the lobby to a conference room or their office as a great time to build rapport. It's a crucial step because more rapport means more trust, which leads to a smoother sales process.

Building rapport can be as simple as asking about someone's weekend, the weather, or their favorite local sports team. For me, being in Wisconsin, the snow and Packers are a can't miss.

## KEY POINTS ABOUT RAPPORT

- Make it about them
- Use social cues when it's time to move on
- Be sincere, don't fake it
- Don't comment about every interesting thing and try to tie it to you

As a general rule, never try to go into the business part of the conversation (depending upon People Types, see Chapter 26) until you've at least made the lead laugh, or had them tell a story about their latest escapades, vacation or work situation. You're going to want to build rapport to a comfortable level before you continue. But don't make it awkward. Be sure to pick up on cues from the person you're meeting with if they want to move the conversation along.

When you're ready to take control of the conversation and move, create a bridge between Rapport (Step 1) and Asking Questions (Step 2). During this time, I recommend reminding the prospect or customer why you're meeting in the first place.

A good transition can look like:

- The reason for my call today is...
- What I'm hoping we can solve today is...
- Here's what I'd like to discuss today...

Quickly summarize why you're there and ask if there's anything they'd like to cover in your conversation. Take control by demonstrating that you're prepared to get down to business. Most people will appreciate your professionalism and preparedness, and you've gained a micro-commitment to move along.

You can never have enough rapport. Seriously, good rapport signals high levels of trust, and you want to be trusted. You'll know you've built good rapport when clients and prospects are sharing personal stories with you, including sending you pictures of their kids playing sports or talking about their father-in-law's illness. For those that are more introverted, it will take time to build rapport. They won't be as open to sharing personal details, but never stop building rapport on lighter professional topics.

## CHAPTER 23

# ASK QUESTIONS AND LISTEN

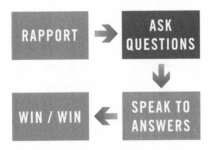

I always think it's funny when salespeople say, "If I could only read the prospect's mind." How silly, you already can. You just need to ask them! The best salespeople are typically the best at asking questions. If you want to be great at sales, this is a step you'll have to master. Of the Four-Part

Sales Method steps, this step is the most critical. You can have a lot going for you, but if you can't ask great questions—you're doomed.

Listen, you can fake a lot of things in the sales process, but you can't fake asking good questions. Good questions can separate you from your competitors and put you into a class of your own. The problem with most salespeople is that they don't want to go deep enough with their questions. Imagine you sell medical devices and you're calling on a clinic that's opening a new location across town. Many salespeople will assume that's all they need to know and not ask much more. They *should* be asking these follow-up questions:

- Why are you opening a new office?
- How'd you choose this location vs. others?
- Will your medical device needs change in this new office?
- How will this impact the business?
- What level of involvement will you have?
- How do you see this impacting the company's future?

And the list of questions goes on and on if you're curious enough. The responses to these questions will give you far greater insight into where your prospect is headed and how you can provide value and sell more medical devices. By asking and listening, you'll earn their trust and repeat business.

You owe it to your prospects to ask great questions and get to the heart of their issues. Think of yourself as their problem solver. They may never have realized how much they're losing out on or could be gaining, and if you ask the right questions and expose that knowledge, you have instant credibility. You can ask these questions because you've built great rapport and your level of trust is high. Remember, if you want someone to be direct and honest with you, you need to be direct and honest with them.

## THE FOUR MAIN MOTIVATIONS OF ASKING QUESTIONS AND LISTENING

1. Gain insight into their wants and needs
2. Verbally articulate and clarify their needs and wants
3. Continue to build trust
4. Move them to a position where they are selling themselves on your product or service

Be prepared for the meeting. Research, and draw off of your past conversations or emails to have an understanding of what your prospect's potential obstacles could be, and how your solution can solve them. While you should walk into the meeting with some understanding, this next interaction either in person or in a conference call or webinar is where you'll want to ask your best questions.

Here's a simple framework that I like to follow when asking questions:

- What's their current situation?
- Where do they want to be?
- What's the risk/reward if they stay in their current situation or migrate to where they want to be?
- How can they benefit from moving to where they want to be?

The more you can get the prospect feeling the divide between their *current* situation and their *desired* situation, the better. The more articulate you can assist in this *desired* situation, the better. You don't just have to appeal to their business needs, but also to an individual's ego, credibility, career aspirations, and peace of mind.

When it comes to structuring your questions, I recommend starting high level and drilling down. Never make assumptions, and if you don't understand something, just ask. People love to talk about themselves, their product, their company, and their systems, so allow them to educate you.

A good rule of thumb is 25 percent talking and 75 percent listening. You should ask questions and take great notes, or listen *very* intently to the answers. Most salespeople want to demonstrate how clever or well prepared they are by helping the prospect answer questions. That's annoying and rude—don't do that. Let the prospect fully speak and get out their entire answer. Once they're done, you can ask a question to gain some clarity, but don't interrupt.

I'm always skeptical if I'm the prospect in this type of conversation and the person I'm meeting with isn't taking notes. It makes me think that they're either not listening or disinterested. So take good notes. It reminds me of the absolute panic I experience anytime I go to a restaurant and the server wants to show off their memory and memorize everyone's order! This may be a cool party trick, but inside I'm super skeptical. Did he get my steak temperature right? Is he positive that he heard that my mother-in-law utterly hates anything spicy? Seriously dude, save us the anxiety and please, please, please write down my order!

Now you might say, "I have a photographic memory." Good for you, here's a ribbon! Even if you have a photographic memory and you can remember the entire conversation, take notes. It shows that you're actively engaged in the conversation and gives me confidence that you're not forgetting my answers and wasting my time.

Summarizing points is a great way to demonstrate that you are, in fact, paying attention and you care about the answer. Using statements like, "Let me make sure I understand you properly. You said that growing sales by 200 percent was your goal this year?" This question and all of its other forms is a great way to build trust in the conversation and the relationship.

In a conversation, most people are just waiting for their turn to talk. Have the restraint and self-control to be present in the conversation and the situation.

This section of asking questions and listening for answers really comes down to how curious you are about your prospect. The best salespeople have a genuine level of curiosity. Every person has a story, and every business has lessons that you could learn. So be curious.

CHAPTER 24

# SPEAK TO ANSWERS

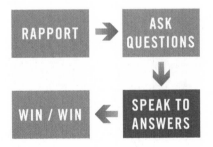

You've built rapport, you've asked questions and listened, now what?

Now is the time to transition from asking questions about their problems and needs, to how you and your service or product can help. Think of it like a doctor's appointment.

Let's say you've had acute pain in your right side for the past few days so you schedule an appointment. For the first half of the conversation, your doctor should be asking how much it hurts, where it hurts, what were you doing when the pain started to happen, etc. She may have you lay down and feel where the pain is. The doctor collects all sorts of information, followed by her opinion and what she's going to do to fix it. She's "speaking to answers."

Speaking to Answers is when you, as a salesperson, need to paint a clear picture of what your prospect's problem is, the downside of them continuing to stay in their current situation, and how you and your solution can be the antidote to what pains them.

You need to go past words and demonstrate the benefits they'll experience from the solution that you'll provide. Appeal to more than just their logic—appeal to their ego. Appeal to the old reptilian part of the brain that wants to be seen as a good leader and a smart executive.

Using our doctor analogy, this is when the doctor says, "Mark, after talking through your symptoms and from my thorough investigation, I believe your appendix is about to rupture. You need to get to surgery or you could face serious infection." The doctor is giving me the specific problem, and how she's going to solve it. That's what Speaking to Answers is all about.

Side note: When I was fourteen, I actually had my appendix removed, despite my dad's misdiagnosis as a stuck fart!

As you're demoing your solution, product, or service, go line by line on how your solution addresses not only their immediate need and problem but how the solution can change their company, life, gain peace of mind, reduce fear, etc.

Throughout your presentation, make sure you're using a form of questions and agreements called **"tie-downs"** Tie-downs are short questions designed to gain small agreements, engage your prospect, and pave the path to commitment. Too often salespeople spend the whole time talking while speaking to answers, which can cause your prospect to tune you out. One way to effectively combat this is through the use of tie-downs.

Here are some examples of tie-downs:

- Does that make sense?
- Do you follow me?
- Are we on the same page?
- Do you know what I mean?
- Aren't they?
- Can't you?
- Isn't it?
- Shouldn't it?
- Won't they?

As useful as they can be, these questions can also backfire if not used as a natural part of the conversation. However, I do believe that through effective use of the tie-downs, you have a better understanding of your prospect.

Avoid buzzwords and clichés. They sound inauthentic and makes you blend into the masses of salespeople that use the word synergy. Also, avoid your internal and industry jargon. That's great that you're a little smarty pants and know it, but if your prospects aren't familiar with the term, it doesn't matter. If you use the jargon and ten-million-dollar words, congrats. You've just created a wall between you and your prospect—not good. Speak and use the language of your prospect, not yours.

Lastly, always remember to answer the question running through your prospect's mind: "What's in it for me?" No one cares about how elegant and smart your product or solution is if you can't make a clear connection to how it will solve their problem. Too many salespeople assume that prospects connect the dots. Let me give you a hint, they're not! You need to make it crystal clear that your solution will solve their problem. In sales, there's no such thing as too much clarity, especially when "speaking to answers."

CHAPTER 25

# WIN-WIN

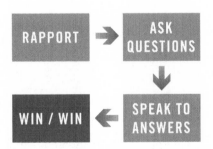

The Win-Win part of selling means creating a commitment to future action. That could mean a purchase if appropriate, or an agreement on the best next action. Regardless of your next step, never leave the site of a meeting or conversation without a firm and agreed upon commitment to a future activity if you can genuinely benefit your prospect.

Now keep in mind you can only move forward to creating a win-win if you've done the following correctly:

- Built a high level of trust in your product, company, and you personally
- Asked questions that exposed their real desire, want, and need
- Spoke to answers that revealed how costly and painful staying in their current situation is
- Created the next logical step in line with what your solution can offer

Creating a win-win means that you either have a commitment of the next step in your buying process or sold them your solution (hooray!!).

During win-win and throughout the sales process there's probably going to be a point when you're going to want to bring up potential roadblocks, hiccups or speed bumps that will inevitably be experienced when using your product or solution. Few things ever go as planned. Quiet that inner voice that's telling you to gloss over this and instead, be honest. Be truthful about what a real win-win is. Expose the potential speed bumps and transparently shine a light on their existence. You're a guide and educator, not a pushy sales rep. It's better to get only one order now, while you build trust and foundation as a key resource for your buyer. Trust me. You'll get more sales in the long run. This is way better than selling them too much or extras they don't need, dooming the relationship for failure from the start.

There are scores of "closing techniques" that have been around since the dark ages of selling. At their core, the vast majority are manipulative. I don't believe in them and it's not something I teach. Creating a win-win is all about finding and creating value. It's the natural progression of the conversation to finish with a confident ask of the prospect to take the next appropriate action.

Creating a win-win isn't something that you force, cajole, or manipulate. Sure, you might get some early and easy wins this way, but if your goal is to build a relationship and form lifelong customers, you need to create a win-win.

# CHAPTER 26

## PEOPLE TYPES

So we've walked through the Four-Part Sales Method of building rapport, asking questions, speaking to answers, and creating a win-win. Now, we're going to discuss a common thread that can be applied to all four parts of the Method. It's not enough to simply go through the motions of the Method. You have to pair it with People Types. It's like Tom without Jerry, Batman without Robin, PB without J. I think you get the point.

These People Types have been developed through years of my observation, in the field selling, and by reading Myers Briggs Assessments, DiSC profiles, and Classical Temperamental Styles. The Classical Temperamental Styles are as old as Socrates and Plato (who were awesome salespeople, by the way). Even thousands of years ago, they realized that not everyone has the same disposition or motivations.

I poured over pages of research and sat through countless workshops and distilled it down to help you sell more. You can go back and read all the books, get all the experience, and attend all the classes, or you can follow along with my model that was built with sales in mind. Caution: People Types are easy to forget to use in sales situations. Why? We get nervous, excited, or both. But if you take time to learn them, you will dramatically increase your confidence and sales success.

Having a deep understanding of People Types is like having the answers to the test. After some time and experience, you'll start to see habits and patterns repeat themselves, making it easier for you to handle and recognize. I've had salespeople who, before People Types, struggled to communicate or get any sales traction. Once they understood people, their whole world changed. They are now able to have much better and productive conversations, and of course sell more! Why?

**Different people need to be communicated to differently.** I told you this wasn't rocket science. But the problem I see with a lot of salespeople is that they get stuck selling to different people the same way. It's the way *they* want to be sold.

You should have processes and structure for how your pitches, calls, and demos go, but you should tailor each customer interaction based on the type of person they are.

People buy for their reasons, not yours. To have the most success in selling, you need to meet prospects and clients at their level. I remember when I first got into selling, I tried for months on end to get an Engineering Manager to buy our solution. I'd offer him lunches, basketball tickets, you name it! It wasn't until I realized that he probably hated having lunch with a practical stranger or being forced into public situations. So, I changed my tune. I met him at his level, providing the facts, figures, and data he was asking for, and that account grew successfully and profitably.

It's critical to understand how people are motivated and how best to communicate with them. Don't overlook this section because you think you "know" people.

I'm going to suggest there are four types of people in the world.

- Party People
- People Pleasers
- Fact Folks
- Bulls

I get it. You're probably thinking, "Out of 7.5 billion people in the world, you can boil everyone down to four types?"

## PEOPLE TYPES

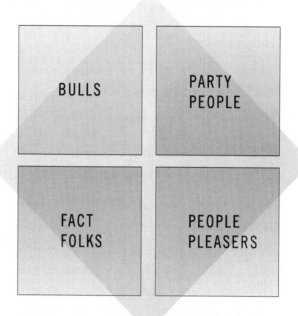

Well, yes and no. People *can* embody more than one type. It's not uncommon for individuals to be primarily Party People, but also be People Pleasers. Furthermore, what one person might be at work can be far different from how they are at home. Even who we are interacting with can change our People Type.

There are a lot of dynamics that come into play when trying to understand People Types, but if you follow these steps, it's easy.

1. Know your type
2. Try your best to determine the kind of person you're meeting with (warning: don't categorize them too quickly)
3. Adapt your communication and selling approach to them
4. Know that circumstances and situations can influence People Types, so don't be shocked if it changes

Remember that "How I am is *not* how you are. How I like to buy is different from how *you* like to buy." Once you truly understand this and can recognize what type of person you're working with, your results can be limitless.

Before we go any further, you need to know which type *you* are. You won't know how to sell the other People Types until you're confident in your own.

## People Types

Try this six-question assessment.

1. What do you eat for breakfast?
   a. Whatever I find in my desk drawer
   b. I bring in donuts for the office
   c. I sit down for half a grapefruit, plain Greek yogurt, and homemade granola
   d. Just black coffee

2. Where do you hang out at a wedding?
   a. I start the conga line
   b. I help put the gifts away and clean up at the end of the night
   c. I usually end up having a quiet conversation at the table with an old friend
   d. I command the conversation by the bar about last weekend's big game

3. What is your desk décor?
   a. My trophy for when I won the office chili cook-off, framed pictures from vacations with friends, a few funny comics
   b. My kid's artwork, framed photos of my pets, and a plant
   c. It's clean and minimal—my pens are neat, there is no dust in sight, and my pictures were hung with a level
   d. My alma mater pennant, MBA diploma, framed photos from past accomplishments

4. When you buy a car, how do you typically feel?
   a. I get so excited! I love the fresh car smell!
   b. I don't want to let the sales rep down
   c. I crunch the numbers and know how much per mile it costs to own and operate the vehicle
   d. Cars are a status symbol—I want to get it over with so I can drive the car down the road

5. What is your ideal vacation style?
   a. I like to go, see, and do! I make it fun no matter where I am!
   b. I usually like to travel with or see friends and family on my vacations
   c. My itinerary is planned well ahead of time
   d. I like exclusive resorts and focus on unique experiences

6. If you could go out to dinner tonight, where would you go?
   a. Any bar, restaurant, or fun spot will do...as long as it's busy
   b. I'm happy to go wherever everyone else wants to go
   c. I prefer the place with the highest Yelp rating
   d. Usually, I end up at the place with the longest line or was the hardest to get into

*Answer key on the next page*

*Answer Key: If you got mostly A's, you're a Party Person. If you got mostly B's, you're a People Pleaser. If you got mostly C's, you're a Fact Folk. If you got mostly D's, you're a Bull.*

Now that you know who you are let's dive into each "people type" further. Because remember, "How I am is *not* how you are. How I like to buy is different from how *you* like to buy."

Here's a quick summary:

**Party People**—Extroverts, chatty, great at a cocktail party, the center of attention, charismatic, perceived as cocky/confident, wants to be seen as likable and successful, buys on feelings

**People Pleasers**—Wants the team to be happy, doesn't like confrontation, hard-pressed to offer an opinion, focused on people, often struggles to decide because they want everyone to be happy and don't want to step on anyone's toes

**Fact Folks**—Detailed, spreadsheets, ROI, buys on evidence/data/facts, not feelings, likes "t's" crossed and "i's" dotted

**Bulls**—Get in line or get out of the way, driven by ego, concerned about success/results and are often perceived that they do not care about anyone else but themselves

# PARTY PEOPLE

Party People are enthusiastic, dynamic, and charismatic. You'll know who these people are at any cocktail party because they're usually the ones having all the fun. They do very well at networking events, or any place there's a large group of people. These individuals are your classic extroverts! They're chatty and they love being the center of attention. Typically, they are in sales and marketing.

They desperately want to be perceived as likable and successful. They often want to be liked by everyone to a fault. They express their opinions and feelings and talk with their hands. They thrive from being recognized for their contribution to helping people.

Party People are great at building rapport and developing relationships. They can get tripped up over the details because usually, they're unconcerned about them. They make decisions based on emotions and gut feelings.

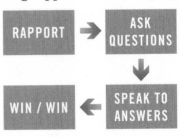

## Rapport Advice for Party People

Keep the conversation enthusiastic, upbeat, and energetic

Don't gloss over building rapport, this is a critical part for them to get to like you

Invite these People Types to lunch, coffee, football games, or networking events

Be liberal with compliments

Let them talk about themselves

## Asking Questions & Listening Advice for Party People

Use open-ended follow-up questions to get them talking and answering in greater detail

Their answers may take you into different tangents so be ready and open to an evolving conversation

You may have to get the conversation back on track with your questions

## Speaking to Answers with Party People

Make it a dialogue, ask for feedback

Tell stories of how this solution or product has helped other companies and people

Demos should be a conversation, with lots of back and forth asking them for advice

Use social proof, so they can see who else uses your product and service

## Win-Win with Party People

Make emotional decisions

Let them talk themselves into your product or solution

Can be more spontaneous, so appeal to their quick decision-making skills

Follow-up frequently to keep the process moving because they often will forget about what their next step is

## WHAT TO AVOID

- Boring them with the details, spreadsheets, and diagrams...they're not paying attention
- Dominating the conversation
- Having low energy or being in a crappy mood

If you're a leader and you manage this type of person:

- Let them express their opinions and feelings
- Make it fun
- Recognize them whenever warranted
- Don't micromanage
- Respect their ideas
- Put them in situations where they'll need to think creatively
- Let them think about the big picture
- Usually work best in teams
- Don't expect them to be detail focused

# PEOPLE PLEASERS

The People Pleaser type is the heart and soul of most organizations. Most of the time they're in HR or customer service. These are the types of people that spend their nights and weekends making cupcakes for the office.

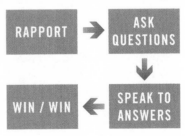

Team morale is incredibly important to them so they organize team lunches and desperately want everyone to be happy! They avoid confrontation at all fronts, even if they know who ate their lunch in the lunchroom. These People Types are focused on people and security.

### Rapport Advice for People Pleasers

Keep the conversation around the people in their lives, including coworkers and family

Know that they may not come around to you on the first interaction, but take your time

Focus on building trust

Be friendly and sincere

### Asking Questions & Listening Advice for People Pleasers

Amplify any problem your solution solves by asking how the issue impacts their employees

Use follow-up questions like "how does that make you feel" or "how does that impact you or your people"

Use empathy when asking questions and thank them for their honest answers

### Speaking to Answers with People Pleasers

Show how your product or solution will make the lives of the people using it better

Don't overwhelm with facts and figures

Show how your solution will bring stability to a situation

Demonstrate in detail the onboarding and support process

### Win-Win with People Pleasers

Keep in mind that they tend to make decisions more slowly

Tie your solution to how it will help their people or customers improve their daily lives

Give them a clear structure of "what happens next and by when"

Use social cred to demonstrate how safe your decision is

## WHAT TO AVOID

- Being too forceful, overbearing or demanding
- Jumping right into your product
- If your demo isn't going well, you won't be able to read them, they'll never say anything because they don't want to rock the boat or offend you
- Being pushy or demanding answers without giving them time to think and process

If you're a leader and you manage this type of person:

- Ask for their help
- Recognize them for a job well done
- Give them the "why" behind any change
- Recognize them for their dependability and ability to finish projects
- Tie the mission into how it will help other people
- Give them time and space to process any changes
- Be friendly, ask them how they're doing and really listen
- Don't forget birthdays or anniversaries
- Put them in situations to help others
- Be concerned about the people in their lives and their home/family situation
- Be open about your family, friends, home situation

## FACT FOLKS

Everyone knows a Fact Folk when they meet them. They're usually in positions of IT, engineering, finance, or operations. This people type is all about the evidence, facts, and data. These individuals tend to be analytical, detail oriented, and are deep thinkers. They could care less about your family, or dog, or the big game that was on last night. They want to get lost in the data and review the ROI, so be prepared to get in the weeds. The more charts, the better! Excel is their BFF.

They are introverted and try to avoid being singled out in a crowd. They often strive for perfection within themselves and their surroundings, which is why their desks, cars, garages, and houses are usually spotless! You know the type, the friend who has every nut and bolt organized in their workshop. Or the friend who's always prepared for anything when your families get together.

These people are all about process, results, and security. They often have the hardest time making a change. They'll weigh all of the options before making a decision and will pour over the data, findings, and results.

## Rapport Advice for Fact Folks

Use an agenda, and let them know what you'd like to cover right away

Don't be offended if they don't want to talk about themselves, use it as a cue to move the conversation ahead

Don't expect to win them over on the very first meeting or call

## Asking Questions & Listening Advice for Fact Folks

Demonstrate in your questions that you've done your homework in preparation of the meeting

When possible, site reference articles and trade publications in your questions

Ask questions that are ROI and numbers-focused

Reassure them you are writing down their questions and will follow-up with detailed answers

## Speaking to Answers with Fact Folks

Lead with the data

Speak in terms of cost savings and ROI, including charts and graphs when necessary

Have the facts behind your facts ready, don't be shocked if they're double checking your math, or asking you how you came up with your numbers, estimates, ROI, etc.

Keep it to the point

Don't embellish or exaggerate

## Win-Win with Fact Folks

Make purchasing your product or solution a logical choice

Layout clear instructions and expectations of the process and follow-through

Use conservative estimates, don't sugarcoat anything

Make sure all of your "t's" are crossed and your "i's" are dotted, any error can lead to an erosion of trust

Give exact dates of delivery and deadlines

## WHAT TO AVOID

- Being unorganized
- Fact Folks like to be right, so don't argue a point
- If you don't know an answer, don't make one up
- Rushing them into decisions
- An overabundance of energy
- Flashy presentations with no substance

If you're a leader and you manage this type of person:

- Trace their contribution to the big picture
- Give clear instructions and a process of what they're going to do, and what's expected
- If you're going to make a change, give them time to process and analyze
- Appeal to their expertise and knowledge
- Recognize them for their attention to detail, craftsmanship, and job well done
- Be careful to recognize them in front of other people; a private recognition may be more of what they're looking for
- Focus on recognizing their work, not them personally...i.e., your work was great vs. you're great
- Let them weigh all their options before a decision needs to be made
- Put them in charge of leading the research and analysis of decisions that need to be made

# BULLS

Get in line or get out of the way. Bulls are driven by ego and concerned about results. These are the type of people that don't let anyone or anything stop them. They see it as a personal challenge when you say, "it can't be done." Bulls love independence and are decisive and goal oriented. They enjoy being in charge of a group since they have leadership qualities and the ambition to get it done. Typically, Bulls are throughout your organization as managers and owners. People who are Bulls who are *not* a manager or owner usually get fired.

Bulls want to see results *now*. They make quick decisions and they want to be in control. Give them the ball and let them run with it.

Don't get too chatty with Bulls because they want to get down to business. They'll love to talk about their alma mater, but could give two shits about where you went to school. Have your facts and figures ready, provide the information in tight formation, and then get the hell out of there.

They're the crazies at your gym who are going after it on the elliptical machine while reading the Wall Street Journal, listening to a podcast, and watching Fox

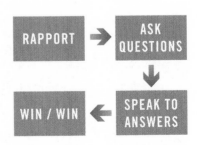

Business. You better keep up, or they'll leave you behind. Recognition and results are the name of the game. People and security...meh.

### Rapport Advice for Bulls

Compliment them on their successes or any other achievement/award/recognition/mention in news they've had

Ask them how they got into the company and how they got into the position they are in

Bulls move fast so get down to business

### Asking Questions & Listening Advice for Bulls

Don't tap dance around a topic—make your questions direct

Bulls like to be challenged, so don't back down—it could just be a test

Hit them with the tough questions right away; you may not get to them later in the conversation

### Speaking to Answers with Bulls

Show how it will make them look like a smart leader and executive

Focus on the big outcome; they don't want to hear features

Keep it tight and concise, allowing them to ask questions and visualize how it will work into their process

Present with executive summaries, have the data ready if they ask for it, but don't lead with mountains of stats and charts

### Win-Win with Bulls

Bulls tend to make decisions confidently, once they've sold themselves, they're in

They like to win, so when you can, give them a small victory on negotiation or deal

Give them the perception that they're in control of this process

## WHAT TO AVOID

- Being meek or timid
- Don't back down from a challenge
- Be able to make decisions quickly
- Overwhelm with data, charts, or diagrams
- Don't spend too much time trying to small talk in the first meeting

If you're a leader and you manage this type of person:

- Channel their ability to get results
- Challenge them whenever possible
- Give them lofty, audacious, long-term goals
- Recognize them for their results
- Paint a picture of where they could go, and what their future could look like
- Involve them on the strategy side of your business
- Know that they want to be their own boss, so don't micromanage
- Move fast, and be able to make decisions quickly
- Channel their drive for recognition and results, recognize them outwardly

These People Types will rub people the wrong way—be ready to do damage control if they're worth it

## SELLING TO OPPOSITES

Ok, so we've done a deep dive into the four People Types. But I want to be sure you understand the most challenging task is to sell to people who are opposite your type.

The People Types images in Chapter 26 highlight that Bulls are the exact opposite of People Pleasers and Party People are the opposite of Fact Folks.

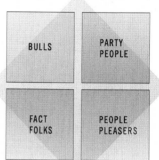

- Bulls have a hard time communicating with People Pleasers.
- People Pleasers have a difficult time communicating with Bulls.
- Party People have a difficult time communicating with Fact Folks.
- Fact Folks have a difficult time communicating and selling to Party People.

If you find your prospect or customer is of your exact opposite People Type, then you'll need to make sure that you're meeting them at their level.

My best advice is to take time before any interaction with them, review the tips in this chapter relevant to their People

Type and practice deep empathy. Think about your communication from their perspective.

I'm not saying that with this tool you'll be able to break down any barriers with opposite People Types magically, but with practice and empathy you'll be amazed at the improvement in communication and results this will yield.

STANDARD 4:
# FOLLOW-UP

I once knew a guy who desperately wanted to move to a particular piece of property. Well, "wanted" to was probably a bit of an understatement. They wanted to move to this particular patch of dirt more than just about anything else. To most people passing by, it was just a rickety old house, on a quiet street. Nothing remarkable stood out about this piece of land. But to this guy's family, it might as well have been the Taj Mahal. It was the perfect piece of property to raise their family, in the right location, with the right amount of mature trees, and to enjoy summers on the lake.

There was just one problem. The property had a house on it, and in that house lived an older gentleman best described as a curmudgeon. He was like a character out of *Grumpy Old Men*. He was rarely home, and let the property fall into disrepair. It was beyond an eyesore, yet held so much potential. That didn't deter the family.

Every fall and spring, like clockwork, they sent a nice letter expressing their interest in the property. At Christmas, they sent a family card or sent cookies. Whenever they saw the old codger, they went out of their way to be conversational. They even brought out the big guns one summer by dropping off a raspberry pie, made from the very raspberries the old man was going to let die on the vine. None of it seemed to work, but they persisted. They persisted for years until one day they got a letter.

The consistent follow-up and creativity finally struck a nerve. He was ready to sell. Conversations were had, paperwork was drawn up, and before it ever went on the market the family was able to buy the property they always dreamed of. At the signing, the old man talked about how he would never have sold his property if it weren't for the family continuing to follow-up.

If raspberry pie and Christmas cards worked for this family to get the land they always wanted, then you better believe it can work for you. Because the new way of selling respects follow-up as much as the actual sale itself.

Creating strong follow-up is one of the easiest ways to increase your sales results. Why? Most salespeople ignore it. In fact, many don't even consider follow-up to be a part of the sales cycle. This means that there's ample opportunity for you to make a positive impact and create a long-term connection between you and your buyer. There is money in the follow-up, but so many of your competitors are blowing it. They're not following up nearly enough, not to mention without any level of creativity.

One of the biggest rules in business, whether you're just starting or have been in your industry for decades, is "Do what you say you'll do." This may sound simple, but don't violate it. You'll instantly lose credibility and that's a tough hill to climb back up.

There is no easier way for prospects to lose all faith in you if you don't follow through on what you say you'll do. If you say you'll follow-up by a specific time and date, do it. Simple as that. Excuses don't cut it. If you can't make the deadline you agreed upon, call them immediately and explain the circumstances. I can't guarantee that they'll still trust you as much as they previously did, but it's better than a no call.

Anyone can be really good in a meeting or demo, but following up is the real indicator for me. Follow-up gives me a window into how you and your business really operate. I put a higher degree of trust in companies that follow-up consistently and creatively over a couple of months time frame—both before and after the sale. But especially after the sale! It shows me that they have their business processes and systems figured out, leading me to a higher level of trust in their product and business.

I've talked to hundreds of business owners and buyers and one of the biggest complaints is that salespeople rarely follow-up. They'll have a good conversation, presentation, or demo. They don't purchase at that given moment or aren't in the market yet, and then poof! They never hear from their salesperson again. Huh? Talk about a missed opportunity!

Don't be that person.

Think about your typical buying cycle. How many people move fully through your purchasing cycle within just one or two interactions? The average sales cycle probably ranges between two months and 12 months. Let's split the difference and say it's six months.

Instead of putting all of your efforts into trying to find buyers that want to buy today, how are you following up with the majority of businesses that will buy within the next six months? Furthermore, how are you following up with the customers who've purchased from you?

Here's what I suggest:

- Be consistent (C)
- Be creative (C)
- Have a plan (P)

## CHAPTER 27

# CCP

Follow-up at all stages in sales must be C, C, and P—consistent, creative, and follow a plan. Let's start with consistency.

"Success isn't always about greatness. It's about consistency. Consistent hard work leads to success. Greatness will come," encourages Dwayne "The Rock" Johnson.

With consistency comes increased interest, and with increased interest comes increased sales.

The world will not come screeching to a halt if you don't follow-up, but if you want to build a reputation that thrives, you need to schedule follow-up and adhere to a consistent schedule.

I recommend carving out several hours each month devoted to following up with your top prospects and clients in a systematized approach.

**Follow-up can be broken down into two categories: active leads *or* passive leads.**

Active leads are anyone currently in your sales process. This could be companies and people that recently received a demo from you, have an agreement or quote, or are awaiting funding/approval to purchase.

Active leads need to be contacted and followed up on more frequently than passive leads. There will be plenty of reason to connect with an active lead—updating pricing, confirming a meeting, providing valuable research or articles, etc. When it comes to active leads, the easiest way to take the guesswork out of what to do by when, and to keep the process moving, is to establish a consistent schedule.

Your consistent schedule can be as simple as every time you have a meeting, you recap your three main takeaways from the meeting, your next steps, and confirm the next agreed upon action with a due date. This can all be sent via email within four hours of your meeting. Then you send a follow-up handwritten note, and if not already, connect on social media preferably LinkedIn.

So your follow-up for a meeting looks something like this:

- Email (include the format above, and send any relevant case studies, etc.)
- Handwritten note
- Add to a weekly drip email campaign
- Connect on social media

Have a workflow like this for demos, lunches, and any other touchpoint that's critical to your sales process. These gestures don't have to be elaborate, but a simple email and a handwritten note can vastly differentiate you from the competition.

On the other hand, passive leads are individuals and companies who aren't in your sales process because they either just completed a purchase, aren't interested at this time, told you to follow-up in six months, or currently use a competitor.

Passive leads can also include people that are good sources of referrals. For example, if you're a mortgage broker, a good lead source for you would be realtors. It would be a smart strategy to remind these passive leads and referral sources every month that you're out there, ready to do business.

With passive leads, there's not going to be as many natural reasons to connect, so you have to make them. The whole point of communicating with passive leads is so that when they have a need, you're the first person they think of. Hopefully, you've established some value, built a bit of trust, and if nothing else you at least have your name in front of them every thirty days or so. Again, consistency!

Now onto the second C—creativity.

You're living and selling in a golden time for follow-up. So many salespeople follow-up in the exact same boring way. The opportunity to blow past your competition has never been better. So, let's start with the most important rule of follow-up. Stop following up to see if they have questions, or to just check-in. This is the most non-value-add way to position yourself as only another commission starved, faceless salesperson. If you want to really separate yourself from the competition, think about how you can provide value to your prospects and customers. How can you provide value in terms of industry knowledge, current market events, and education?

Salespeople have a tremendous opportunity to be the eyes and ears for a prospect or a customer. Just think, if you're active in your channel, you know about trends, who's doing what, and politics/news shaping your industry. I just listed the lowest of the hanging fruit. Remember you want to be memorable and stand out from the general masses.

Here's a list of some creative ideas sure to stand out from the crowd, and keep you top of mind for your prospect:

- Send books about your prospect's industry, market, or personal development
- Send an industry-related magazine or article
- Send a business newspaper article that they could benefit from
- Coffee, people love coffee
- Send an obscure holiday card (National Taco Day is October 4th!!)
- Send food, or a gift card to a local restaurant or coffee shop
- Send a pen if they have a deal waiting to be signed
- Photoshop their face onto a popular industry publication
- Send another handwritten note
- Send them a postcard from your last vacation or conference you attended
- Invite them to a local event
- Send a simple note of thanks
- Highlight a client for that month

For both passive and active leads, I strongly suggest creating a weekly or monthly email series. This may seem intimidating, but there are simple and free tools you can use to stay relevant and top of mind with active and passive candidates alike. Done is better than perfect, and you always keep working to make your email follow-up more creative too. Just make sure it's consistent and actually occurs!

Last, have a follow-up plan. Sketch it out and stick to it. Here are some examples or ideas to get your brain going.

| Month | What's Inside |
| --- | --- |
| January | Resolution Journal |
| February | Chocolate |
| March | Classic Business Book |
| April | Coffee Mug or Gift Card |
| May | Golf Balls |
| June | Helpful Magazine Article |
| July | Book Relating to Your Industry |
| August | Blank Journal |
| September | Postcard from Your Town |
| October | Halloween Candy |
| November | Handwriten Note of Thanks |
| December | Holiday Card or Children's Holiday Book |

Sales and follow-up don't have to be hard. You don't have to be the one with the most industry knowledge, you just have to keep showing up. That's what follow-up is—consistency, creativity, and having a plan. CCP.

When you break it down and strip away all the crap that most gurus and sales training companies have been pushing for decades, you'll conclude that people want to be treated like people. That's your job, with all the tools and processes I've talked about in these pages. It's your job to turn the material into action and to be a human while doing so.

Think of how you'd treat a friend and sell to them accordingly. It doesn't have to be that hard.

Follow-up is where the gold is buried. Your peers and competition are going to overlook this area, but not you. The plan above takes commitment and work in order to be effective in its execution.

It's taken me many attempts and iterations along the way to find what works, and scrap what doesn't. Follow-up is a lot like eating healthy, drinking plenty of water, or working out daily. You won't see results overnight.

What I can guarantee you though is that over time, with some consistency, you'll have prospects and clients alike buy from you, and refer you to more business because of your consistent and creative follow-up. Stay committed, and don't overlook the follow-up.

# CONCLUSION

**We didn't come this far only to get this far.**

I know what happens after people read books. They dog-ear a few pages, maybe highlight a few sections, and promise to implement some of the ideas next week or "soon."

The lessons that I share in this book are not for entertainment value. They are lessons for you to accelerate sales, business, and life, so you don't make the same stumbles and mistakes that I did.

As Jim Rohn says, "If someone tells me that the eggs are rotten, I'm not going to make an omelet and find out, I'll just take their word for it."

Take my word for it. You need to implement these tactics

into your business today. There are far too many businesses that are just one hiccup in the economy from being out of business. And a lot of their problems could be solved by having a solidified, aggressive sales process.

I know it won't be easy. I know that breaking your status quo is one of the most challenging things in the world. It takes real guts to set a standard of sales for your team by implementing the tactics and strategies discussed in this book. It's just as tricky if you're trying to set a standard for yourself. But I believe our most significant breakthroughs are on the other side of the uncomfortable and the unknown.

When I was a boy, my dad recorded my fake commercials pitching paper scratch pads with the help of my younger sister. I rewatched them on VHS this past Christmas and man, they made me smile (and also made me realize, I've been at this sales thing for a while!).

When I was in high school, my science teacher, Mrs. Peters, told me that I probably wouldn't amount to much. When I was *also* in high school, a friend's dad told me, "Evans, you're gonna go places" while drinking a Scotch and grilling steak. Goes to show you, people in this world will try to tear you down or build you up.

But hear this—it's not up to them. It's *only* up to you. Other people will come and go, but you're the only one responsible for the outcome. You're the only one who knows the trials and tribulations you've been through. You're the only one who knows the mountains you've climbed and the obstacles you've had to overcome.

Everyone I've met has a story of overcoming obstacles of all sizes, each story significant in its own right because it made you *you*.

Aristotle says, "Choice not chance, determines destiny."

But if there's one thing I can leave you with it's this. You are in control of where you want to be. No matter your company, product, location, commission—you have the power to improve your life and career if you really want to. This book doesn't have all the answers, but it's a guide and it can be your start.

The real answers lie deep within each of us. How bad do you want it?

You deserve an amazing life. It's not reserved for someone else. You can be the hero of your own story.

So, get out of your own way. Stop doubting yourself and just do the work. Pick up the phone, send the email, stop the social media lurking, and do what you know you need to do.

*Do* it...and not only when you want to or only the stuff you like. Do the hard work.

If you're reading this, you're in a better position than 99 percent of the world. Be grateful for the opportunity that lies ahead of you. If you're healthy, you're blessed. If you have a family, you're blessed. If you're safe, you're blessed. Don't waste away opportunities.

There's gold in these chapters, but it's not a get rich quick scheme. This is a long-term campaign that starts with you.

You must win the victory over yourself. The tough days are temporary, trust me, I've been there. The pain of regret, of knowing that you could have given more, will stay with you forever. There's no escaping it, so don't live a life of regret.

You can do this. You can make this happen. You can raise your standards. You can build a sales system that generates seven-plus figures. I don't care if you've been a screwup and underperformer your whole life. You're only a few good decisions away from being an entirely different person. Just imagine, your life and business could radically change in the next six months based on the choices you make now. Don't back down, hold back, play small, or think your dreams are out of reach. You can do this. I believe in you.

> *"The cave we fear to enter holds the treasure we seek."*
> —Joseph Campbell

# TAKEAWAYS

## STANDARD 1: MINDSET

**Ten beliefs crucial to the foundation for success.**

- I am disciplined.
- I focus on results, not methods.
- I ignore the "urgent" and concentrate on what's important.
- I have clarity about my scorecard.
- I am authentically myself. You be You.
- I am enthusiastic.
- I lean into the grind of sales.
- I push myself to grow via my mentor, books, and the people I surround myself with.
- I know my Big 5 and look at my Dreamboard daily.
- I believe in abundance.

## STANDARD 2: PREP WORK

**Framework and preparation that makes selling easy.**

- I know my Funnel Math numbers.
- I stick to an Ideal Day and commit to my Almighty Power Hour.
- I confidently Know Thy Buyer.
- I have solid answers to the Sink or Swim Test.
- I practice the Triangle Drill.
- I am my best Social Self.

## STANDARD 3: SELLING

**The Playbook, Sales Method, and People Types that are the engine of Seven Figure Sales.**

- I use the elements of my Playbook every day without fail.
- I start the Sales Method by building rapport.
- I ask questions and then shut up and listen.
- I speak to answers to ensure understanding.

- I create a win-win for both sides.
- I don't assume someone else's People Type is the same as my own.
- I adapt my Sales Method approach to match my audience.

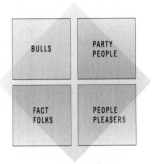

## STANDARD 4: FOLLOW-UP

**Creative, consistent, and planned follow-up—the ultimate differentiator.**

- I have monthly and annual follow-up plans for prospects and my customers.
- I am creative in how I follow-up.
- I am consistent when I do it.

# RESOURCES

## Introduction

Robbins, Tony. Twitter Post. November 21, 2017, 12:43 p.m. https://twitter.com/tonyrobbins/status/933043277175013376

## Chapter 4

Willink, Jocko. *Discipline Equals Freedom: Field Manual*. St. Martin's Press, 2017.

## Chapter 7

Carnegie, Dale. *How to Win Friends & Influence People*. Simon & Schuster, 1937.

Drucker, Peter. *The Practice of Management*. Harper & Row, 1954.

## Chapter 9

Justice Potter Stewart's famous statement originates from the 1964 Supreme Court Case, *Jacobellis v. Ohio*.

Tracy, Brian. *The Psychology of Selling*. Thomas Nelson, 2004.

## Chapter 10

Belfort, Jordan. Twitter Post. April 28, 2017, 11:05 a.m. https://
twitter.com/wolfofwallst/status/857989107959681024

Parcells, Bill. "Bill Parcells: On The Couch." Interview with
Correspondent Rebecca Leung. *CBS 60 Minutes.* August 28,
2003.

https://www.cbsnews.com/news/bill-parcells-on-the-couch/

## Chapter 11

Jones, Charlie T. *The People You Meet and the Books You Read.*
Brolga, 1995.

*The Holy Bible, New International Version.* Biblica, 2011.

## Chapter 12

Dreamboard or Vision Boards are popularized by people
like Oprah Winfrey and *The Secret.* My former boss, Tim
Schmidt, gets credit for the four-quadrant categories.

Polish, Joe. Twitter Post. June 19, 2018, 4:20 p.m. https://twitter.
com/ilmpodcast/status/1009184095954440192

*The Holy Bible, New International Version.* Biblica, 2011.

## Chapter 15

Sir Isaac Newton's First Law of Motion, aka law of inertia,
comes from his *Principia Mathematica Philosophiae
Naturalis* published in 1686.

## Chapter 16

Hill, Napoleon. *The Prosperity Bible: The Greatest Writings of All
Time on the Secrets to Wealth and Prosperity.* Penguin, 2007.

## Chapter 18

Vecsey, George. "Wooden as a Teacher: The First Lesson Was
Shoelaces." *The New York Times,* June 4, 2010.

https://www.nytimes.com/2010/06/05/sports/ncaabasketball/
05wizard.html

## Section 4

"The Man in the Arena" is a famous passage from a speech given by former President Theodore Roosevelt in Paris in 1910 called "Citizenship in a Republic."

## Chapter 27

Johnson, Dwayne. Twitter Post. June 8, 2012, 6:17 a.m. https://
twitter.com/therock/status/211054285432160257

# ACKNOWLEDGMENTS

There was no shortage of people that inspired, conspired, and helped me throughout this process. There are countless mentors whom this book is dedicated to that I'll talk about in further chapters. Their lessons, insight, and advice have shaped my professional career and my philosophy on sales.

To my parents, Mary Kay and Terry for having it all. They bought and built a business all while raising four kids. If it wasn't for their untold sacrifices, and dedication to their piece of the American Dream, I have no idea where I'd be today. They loved and supported me even when I didn't deserve it. Thank you.

To my three sisters, Carla, Kate and Beth, who have laughed at all my jokes since birth, and who've given me the confidence that is a hallmark of my life. I'm grateful for our relationship, the memories and the times we've died laughing together.

To my in-laws, Bruce and Donna. While many wouldn't think of putting their in-laws in their dedication, I'm proud to. I am so fortunate to have such a close relationship with you two. Your support has been unwavering.

To my two daughters, Nina and Mae. This book is a message on sales, but the book at its core is a message to you. I hope you hear, loud and clear, that anything is possible for you both. Packed inside you are all of the promises, hopes, and dreams one father could possibly have. You two make me so proud. I hope I've made you proud.

And lastly, but most importantly, to my wife Katie. I never wanted to write a book. It was not on my radar, was not something I had time to do and was definitely not something I wanted to do for fun. I came up with just about every excuse I could. You knew better. You knew it was all out of fear. Fear of the unknown, fear of taking a chance, and fear of failing. And above the noise, there was you.

You believed in me before I believed in myself. When I doubted my experience, education, skill, or success, you were there to remind me. You have never wavered in your support or encouragement throughout our entire relationship. You've pushed me beyond my shallow limits and have made my life far richer than I could have ever imagined.

It's hard to write this without getting emotional. Your quiet toil made this book. Your stamina to edit page after page, attentive to even the tiniest detail amazes me. Your vision for this book, our family, and business has been transformative. The countless hours with one glass of wine, a snack, and proofing this book is an image I'll never forget. And it's a sacrifice I don't have the words to thank you for. This is our book and it happened because of you.

# ABOUT THE AUTHOR

Mark Evans might be the most enthusiastic person you'll ever meet. His love of sales, life, and the game of business is infectious. He believes that at its very core, sales doesn't have to be manipulative or sleazy. In fact, Mark believes it's the greatest job in the world. He's helped multiple companies and individuals reach the seven-figure sales mark and beyond. At markpatrickevans.com, Mark writes about the new way of selling, and sales leadership. Mark and his wife Katie live in Wisconsin with their two daughters, Nina and Mae.

Made in the USA
Middletown, DE
23 December 2019